# AIR CAMPAIGN

# BATTLE OF THE ATLANTIC 1939–41

RAF Coastal Command's hardest fight against the U-boats

**MARK LARDAS**          ILLUSTRATED BY EDOUARD A. GROULT

OSPREY PUBLISHING
Bloomsbury Publishing Plc

Kemp House, Chawley Park, Cumnor Hill, Oxford OX2 9PH, UK
29 Earlsfort Terrace, Dublin 2, Ireland
1385 Broadway, 5th Floor, New York, NY 10018, USA
Email: info@ospreypublishing.com

OSPREY is a trademark of Osprey Publishing Ltd

First published in Great Britain in 2010
Transferred to digital print in 2024

A catalogue record for this book is available from the British Library.

Print ISBN: 978 1 4728 3603 8
ePub: 978 1 4728 3602 1
ePDF: 978 1 4728 3601 4
XML: 978 1 4728 3604 5

Maps by www.bounford.com
3D BEVs by Paul Kime
Diagrams by Adam Tooby
Index by Nick Hayhurst
Typeset by PDQ Digital Media Solutions, Bungay, UK
Printed and bound in India by Replika Press Private Ltd.

24 25 26 27    10 9 8 7 6 5 4 3 2

**The Woodland Trust**
Osprey Publishing supports the Woodland Trust, the UK's leading woodland conservation charity.

**www.ospreypublishing.com**
To find out more about our authors and books visit our website. Here you will find extracts, author interviews, details of forthcoming events and the option to sign-up for our newsletter.

**Author's Note:**
The following abbreviations indicate the sources of the illustrations used in this volume:
AC – Author's Collection
LOC – Library of Congress, Washington, D.C.
USNHHC – United States Navy Heritage and History Command

**Author's Dedication:**
To my father-in-law, William Potter, who died in December 2018. He was a World War II veteran, a professional astronomer, an amateur historian and always a gentleman. I will miss his advice, which was always good.

# CONTENTS

# INTRODUCTION

**'The only thing that ever really frightened me during the war was the U-boat peril.'**

Winston Churchill, *Their Finest Hour* (*The Second World War* Volume 2)

History is always obvious in retrospect. Yet when occurring, its path is less certain. In 1938–39, no one really worried about the U-boat peril. Virtually all navies viewed submarines as adjuncts to the battle fleet. They were to be used for scouting, and to attack enemy warships prior to naval battles. The submarine was widely seen as an outdated weapon against merchant shipping.

Britain believed convoys and ASDIC (what Britain called sonar) would neutralize the submarine threat. Even in Germany the Kriegsmarine's commander, Erich Raeder, considered U-boats auxiliary to surface warships. They failed in World War I, and defences against them had only improved since then. Luftwaffe commander Hermann Göring believed U-boats (and the rest of the Kriegsmarine) were superfluous. Aircraft could replace them. Only Karl Dönitz, who commanded Germany's U-boats, believed they were a war-winning weapon.

Everyone, except Dönitz and his submarine commanders, was surprised at the effectiveness of the U-boat. Sonar proved less effective than the British believed it to be. Surface attack made the U-boat invisible to sonar, especially at night. Wolf-pack tactics overwhelmed convoy escorts. At the war's end, Dönitz, who led the Kriegsmarine's U-boat arm through most of the war, was Nazi Germany's commander-in-chief, a testimony to the role played by the U-boat.

Politics kept Dönitz from unleashing his U-boats against Allied merchant shipping during the first few months of the war. Initially, Adolf Hitler insisted Germany adhere to Article 22 of the 1930 London Naval Treaty, which required submarines to warn unarmed merchant ships before sinking them (this became known as the London Submarine Protocol). Faulty German torpedoes in the war's first year further limited U-boat success. Even after Hitler permitted unrestricted submarine warfare in August 1940, the limited number of available U-boats during the 'Happy Time' that followed kept the damage they did within acceptable levels for Britain and its allies. The U-boat had not proved the war-winning weapon Dönitz hoped it would be during the first two years of the war.

Britain possessed the major piece of the solution to the U-boat peril right from the start of the Battle of the Atlantic: the anti-submarine aircraft. Used assiduously and effectively in the first months of the war, aircraft could have ended the Battle of the Atlantic in its first year with Nazi Germany abandoning a U-boat campaign their top leaders had been unenthusiastic about when the war started.

There was no more potent threat to U-boats than aircraft. If U-boats were barracudas, slashing at schools of merchant ships, then aircraft were eagles, capable of ripping into a barracuda from above and carrying it away. Even when aircraft could not attack, they could observe their prey and call other hunters to the spot.

In World War I, aircraft contributed as much to defeating the U-boat as did arming merchantmen and convoys. Aircraft forced U-boats to submerge, limiting mobility and destroying their effectiveness. It was the main reason everyone assumed the U-boat was outdated. Aircraft in 1914–18 were primitive, barely able to stay aloft, but by the 1930s the wood and canvas kites had been replaced by all-metal monoplanes capable of carrying a ton or more of weapons.

Britain's leaders bungled this opportunity, failing to build an adequate aerial anti-submarine capability. There were too few aircraft assigned to carry out maritime patrols; most of those

Karl Dönitz was a captain when 1939 began. By the war's end he was a Grossadmiral (Admiral of the Fleet) and became Hitler's successor, largely because of his skill at doing what was considered impossible: using the U-boat against British merchant shipping. (AC)

assigned were either obsolescent, incapable of carrying a sufficient bomb-load or lacking endurance. When the war started, the primary focus of Britain's maritime patrol aircraft was protection of Britain's seaborne trade from surface raiders. Submarines were viewed as unlikely to pose a serious problem.

Britain had almost no effective weapons that aircraft could use against submarines. Those few that were effective could only be carried by the largest maritime aircraft, a small fraction of total available aircraft. The bombs the aircraft most commonly used for maritime patrol could carry would not damage a U-boat, even with a direct hit. The result was that both sides were fighting a battle for which neither had prepared, yet one that would make the struggle's winner the victor of the war. Instead of ending in 1940, the Battle of the Atlantic continued from the first day of World War II until Germany's surrender in May 1945.

Nicholas Monsarrat fought that war as an officer on a Royal Navy corvette. In his magnificent novel of the Battle of the Atlantic, *The Cruel Sea*, he described the early years of the battle as 'like a game of hide-and-seek played by a few children in an enormous rambling garden … some of the children were vicious and cruel, and pinched you when you were discovered.' While Monsarrat's view of the war was from the bridge of a surface warship, it was little different for the aircrew flying aircraft seeking U-boats, or the U-boat crews watching for aircraft. Both sides could 'pinch' hard in the right circumstances.

Both the Allies and the Axis spent the period covered in this book learning to fight the Battle of the Atlantic. The Germans perfected their weapons and tactics against their primary target – merchant shipping – while trying to cope with the threat posed by aircraft. They also worked desperately to increase U-boat production, seeking to raise their numbers to decisive quantities.

Similarly, Britain developed aircraft capable of effectively hunting U-boats, munitions capable of sinking U-boats, systems (such as radar, but also signal intelligence and radio direction finding) capable of finding U-boats and tactics capable of destroying them. They were aided in minor ways during the first eight months of the war by France, and during the last six months of 1941 by the United States, but it was almost entirely an all-British effort.

By the end of December 1941, Britain had finally assembled all the tools to conduct an effective aerial offensive against the U-boat peril. But in late 1941, Germany finally succeeded in increasing U-boat production to war-winning numbers. Additionally, the entrance of the United States into the war following the Japanese attack on Pearl Harbor both expanded the battlefield and vastly changed resources available for the Battle of the Atlantic.

The climactic battles would be fought in 1942 and 1943. But they could not have been fought without the foundations laid between 1939 and 1941. This is the story of the building of those foundations.

# CHRONOLOGY

## 1935
**18 June** Anglo-German Naval Agreement signed, permitting Germany to build U-boats.

**29 June** Kriegsmarine commissions U-1, its first U-boat.

## 1936
**14 July** Coastal Command established.

**12 August** U-27, first Type VII U-boat, commissioned.

## 1937
**30 July** Royal Navy assigned responsibility for control of all carrier-based aircraft.

**16 August** Air Marshal Sir Frederick Bowhill takes command of Coastal Command.

## 1938
**23 June** The British Purchasing Commission signs a contract with Lockheed for the delivery of 200 of its Hudson bombers by December 1939.

Originally Hudsons were shipped to Britain in pieces, aboard ships. They then needed to be assembled and tested, as shown here, delaying delivery to operational squadrons. Later Hudsons were flown across the Atlantic, cutting delivery time. (AC)

## 1939

**24 May** Transition of carrier aircraft to Royal Navy control completed.

**19 August** Dönitz sorties 19 U-boats into the North Sea and Atlantic Ocean in anticipation of the start of World War II.

**24 August** Coastal Command begins patrols of the North Sea and English Channel.

**25 August** Dönitz sends another 19 U-boats into the Atlantic in anticipation of the start of hostilities.

**1 September** Germany invades Poland.

**3 September** Britain and France declare war on Germany.

**17 September** HMS *Courageous* sunk by U-29 while on anti-submarine patrol in the Western Approaches.

## 1940

**January** Mk I Air-to-Surface radar first used on Coastal Command aircraft (Hudsons).

**30 January** First U-boat 'kill' credited to Coastal Command, when a 228 Squadron Short Sunderland forces the previously-damaged U-55 to scuttle.

**9 April** Germany invades Denmark and Norway.

**13 April** Britain occupies the Faroe Islands.

**19 April** Germans begin operating U-boats from Norwegian ports.

**10 May** Britain occupies Iceland.

**10 May** Germany invades the Low Countries and France.

**26 May–4 June** Evacuation of BEF from France.

**8 June** Allies withdraw last forces from Norway; German control complete.

**12 June** First wolf pack organized, Wolf Pack Prien, seven U-boats coordinating to attack Convoy HX-47.

**22 June** France surrenders. Germany occupies Channel Islands and the maritime provinces of France.

**July** Mk II ASV radar enters operation.

**1 July** U-26 scuttled after depth charging by corvette HMS *Gladiolus* and bombs from a 10 Squadron Sunderland.

**7 July** U-boats begin operating out of French Atlantic ports, with the arrival of U-30 at Lorient.

**31 July** First Coastal Command aircraft arrive in Iceland – 98 Squadron, flying Fairey Battles.

**August** Fw 200 Condors begin anti-shipping and maritime reconnaissance operations out of Bordeaux.

**17 August** Hitler declares a total blockade of the British Isles. Unrestricted submarine warfare begins.

**September** Construction of first French submarine pens begins.

**September** U-boat command headquarters moves to Paris.

**4 September** Three Italian submarines enter Bordeaux, starting operations against Allied shipping in the Atlantic.

**9 October** First Italian submarine leave Bordeaux on a war patrol.

**November** U-boat command headquarters moves to Lorient

Dönitz inspects a U-boat crew prior to pre-war exercises. Dönitz encouraged camaraderie between U-boat officers and enlisted sailors, building *esprit de corps* within the U-boat arm. (AC)

## 1941

**1 January** A squadron of Hudsons and one of Sunderlands are sent to Iceland to conduct long-range anti-submarine patrols.

**15 January** 95 Squadron Sunderlands are sent to Freetown, Sierra Leone.

**23 January** 250lb depth charge available for use.

**5 March** First operational delivery of the Consolidated PBY Catalina to Coastal Command.

**6 March** Winston Churchill issues his 'Battle of the Atlantic Directive'.

**24 March** 95 Squadron begins operations out of Freetown, Sierra Leone.

**15 April** The Royal Navy assumes operational control of Coastal Command.

**May** Barrier search patrols initiated in Bay of Biscay and Iceland/Faroes gap.

**June** 200 Squadron (Hudsons) begins operations in Gambia.

**June** 1st U-boat Flotilla transfers to Brest.

**2 June** 120 Squadron, equipped with Consolidated Liberator Is, established at RAF Nutts Corner, Northern Ireland.

**14 June** Air Marshal Sir Philip Joubert de la Ferté takes charge of Coastal Command.

**17 June** HMS *Audacity*, the first Royal Navy escort carrier, is commissioned.

**7 July** Defence of Iceland transferred to the United States.

**August** United States sends VP-73 and VP-74 Squadrons to Iceland; begins anti-U-boat patrols in Neutrality Zone.

**25 August** U-452 sunk by HMS *Vascama* after being damaged by a 209 Squadron Catalina out of Iceland.

**27 August** U-570 surrenders to Coastal Command aircraft.

**September** Coastal Command HQ in West Africa established at White House.

**12 September** HMS *Audacity* escorts its first convoy, OG 74, outbound from Britain to Gibraltar.

**9 October** 9th U-boat Flotilla established at Brest.

**22 October** Coastal Command relinquishes control of West Africa operations to West African Command.

**30 November** Coastal Command Armstrong Whitworth Whitley on Bay of Biscay patrol makes first successful radar-guided attack on a U-boat, damaging U-71.

**7 December** United States attacked by Japan at Pearl Harbor and other bases in the Pacific.

**11 December** Germany declares war on the United States.

**21 December** HMS *Audacity* sunk by U-751.

**21 December** U-451 sunk off Tangiers by an 812 Squadron Fairey Swordfish in the first successful radar-guided night attack.

# ATTACKERS' CAPABILITIES
## The Cinderella service

Great Britain began World War II with inadequate anti-submarine aircraft, inadequate facilities and infrastructure for the anti-submarine aircraft it did have, and weapons and tactics largely incapable of sinking U-boats. It was forced to withdraw Royal Navy aircraft carriers from anti-submarine efforts within a month of the war's outbreak.

Both Coastal Command and the Fleet Air Arm (FAA) received a lower priority for new equipment and facilities aimed at anti-submarine warfare than Bomber Command for strategic bombing. Both initially prioritized anti-shipping ahead of anti-submarine efforts.

It took two years of warfare for Britain to develop an effective aerial anti-U-boat force. As 1941 started, Britain had the types of aircraft and weapons that could effectively attack U-boats, and was developing the necessary bases and infrastructure for its aerial U-boat campaign. As 1941 ended, Britain finally knew how to effectively attack U-boats from the air.

The Avro Anson was the most numerous bomber in Coastal Command when World War II started. However, it was incapable of carrying a bomb large enough to seriously damage a U-boat, and ended the war without sinking any. (AC)

## Aircraft

Coastal Command used both landplanes and seaplanes as maritime patrol aircraft. Maritime patrol is a more accurate term than anti-submarine aircraft because Coastal Command's primary focus in September 1939 was blockading German-bound merchant ships, and monitoring and attacking German surface warships. Hunting U-boats was initially a low priority, and did not become Coastal Command's primary emphasis until after June 1940. Aware of the inadequacy of their aircraft, Coastal Command was upgrading them when the war began, both through domestic production and purchase abroad. The chief aircraft types used between 1939 and 1941 included the following:

**Anson:** The main maritime patrol aircraft used by Coastal Command in 1939, the land-based Avro Anson equipped nine Coastal Command squadrons in September 1939. First flown in 1935, by 1939 the Anson was approaching obsolescence. It normally carried two 100lb bombs and two .303 machine guns, with one in a dorsal turret and one fixed forward.

The Lockheed Hudson was the backbone of Coastal Command through the war's early years. Equipped with an effective bombsight, and sophisticated bomb release gear, it could drop a stick of bombs at preset intervals. (AC)

Slow, it had an endurance of 4½ hours and lacked the range to make a round trip to Norway from Britain. Despite its shortcomings, it remained in the Coastal Command inventory through the first 20 months of the war. Ansons sank no U-boats over the course of the war.

**Hudson**: Realizing the Anson's weaknesses, Coastal Command purchased the Lockheed Hudson, a military modification of Lockheed's Model 14 Super Electra land airliner. An order for 200 Hudsons to be delivered by December 1939 was placed in June 1938. Delivery started in February 1939 and the first Hudson-equipped squadron became operational in May.

The Hudson could carry 1,000lb of bombs, cruised at 165 knots and had a six-hour endurance with a range of 1,000nm (nautical miles). It also had a sophisticated bombsight and bomb-release gear, allowing spaced release of the payload. It became Coastal Command's main anti-U-boat aircraft between 1939 and 1941, with over 1,500 serving during that period. Hudsons captured U-570 in August 1941, and ended the war having killed or sharing credit for killing 25 more U-boats.

**Wellington, Whitley, Hampden**: Three twin-engine RAF medium bombers developed in the mid-1930s, these were Bomber Command's front-line bombers when the war began. By late 1940 they were being superseded by a new generation of four-engine heavy bombers. As the new bombers came online, the older aircraft were shifted to other duties, including maritime patrol. All three had long range (over 1,400nm), could carry at least 4,000lb of bombs and had space for extra equipment, such as radar or (eventually) Leigh lights. Coastal Command had four squadrons equipped with these aircraft as 1941 ended, some on loan from Bomber Command. The Whitley first saw service in anti-submarine duty in late 1940, joined by Vickers Wellington squadrons in 1941. While Coastal Command primarily used the Handley Page Hampden as a torpedo bomber, it was occasionally used for anti-submarine patrols. Although these aircraft sank no U-boats in the war's first two years, by 1945 they were credited with destroying 27 enemy submarines.

**Liberator**: The Consolidated Liberator was a four-engine bomber built in the United States. It had a range of 1800nm, could carry 2,700lb of bombs that distance and was capable of staying aloft for ten hours. It was heavily armed; with 14 .303 machine guns in British versions.

It could be fitted with radar, had space for relief crew and was easy to fly once airborne. The ideal maritime patrol aircraft, it was also an ideal day bomber (with a bombload of 8,000lb). In wrestling matches with Bomber Command, Coastal Command almost always lost: of the first 120 Liberators delivered to Britain, only 17 were assigned to Coastal Command.

These aircraft were available because they were ordered by France in 1939, and the order transferred to Britain when France surrendered. The first Liberator-equipped squadron became operational in July 1941, assigned to Northern Ireland and long-range patrols over the North Atlantic. (It would be joined in late November 1941 by a squadron of Boeing B-17 Fortress Is, an export version of the four-engine B-17, similarly converted to maritime patrol aircraft.) Liberators sank no U-boats between 1939 and 1941. The last half of 1941 saw them influence the battlefield, despite small numbers, most notably in discouraging wolf-pack attacks in their patrol areas. Liberators would sink or assist in sinking 72 U-boats between 1942 and 1945.

**Sunderland**: The Short Sunderland was a four-engine monoplane flying boat that entered service in September 1938. Designed for maritime patrol, it was the only monoplane seaplane in RAF service when World War II started. It carried up to 2,000lb of bombs or depth charges in an internal bomb bay, mounted on racks that ran in and out of the side of the aircraft on rails under the wing. It was heavily armed, carrying 16 .303 and two .50 calibre machine guns. With a range of 1,700nm, it could remain aloft for nearly 13 hours.

The Sunderland was Britain's most capable anti-submarine aircraft until the Liberators entered service. Their main problem was a lack of numbers. Production in the early months of the war was typically just five per month. This was difficult to increase due to Short's production of Bomber Command's first four-engine bomber, the Stirling, which had production priority. (Its total production run was only 750 aircraft.) Additionally, the Sunderland required more ground maintenance than two-engine patrol craft, further limiting air time. Sunderlands were credited with the destruction of two U-boats in 1939–40, and sank another 24 later in the war.

The only modern flying boat available to Coastal Command in 1939 was the four-engine Short Sunderland. Introduced operationally in 1938, it had outstanding range, heavy defensive armament and a large bombload. (AC)

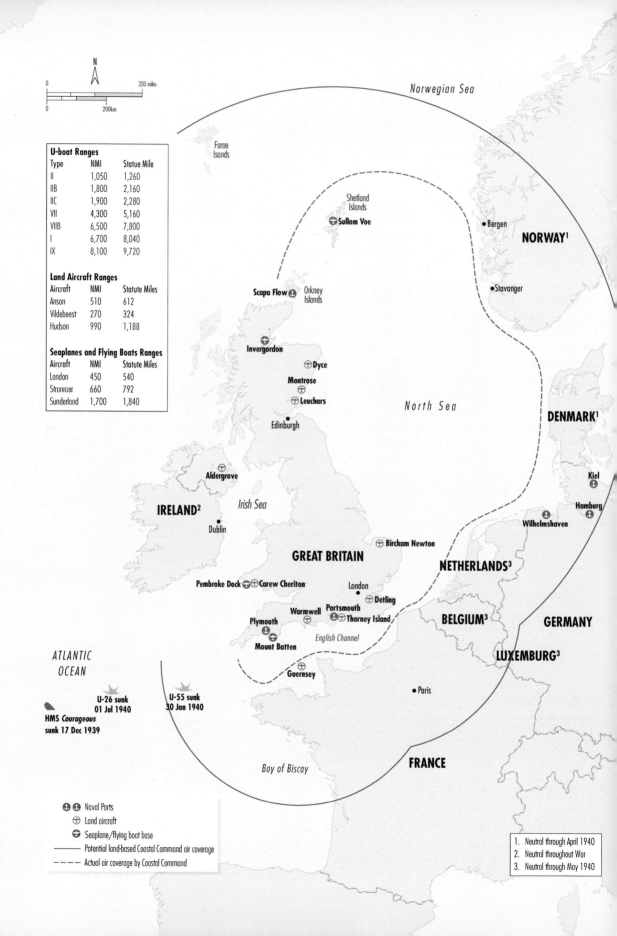

N

| 0 | | | 200 miles |
| 0 | | 200km | |

**U-boat Ranges**

| Type | NMI | Statue Mile |
|------|------|------------|
| II | 1,050 | 1,260 |
| IIB | 1,800 | 2,160 |
| IIC | 1,900 | 2,280 |
| VII | 4,300 | 5,160 |
| VIIB | 6,500 | 7,800 |
| I | 6,700 | 8,040 |
| IX | 8,100 | 9,720 |

**Land Aircraft Ranges**

| Aircraft | NMI | Statute Miles |
|----------|------|--------------|
| Anson | 510 | 612 |
| Vildebeest | 270 | 324 |
| Hudson | 990 | 1,188 |

**Seaplanes and Flying Boats Ranges**

| Aircraft | NMI | Statute Miles |
|----------|------|--------------|
| London | 450 | 540 |
| Stranraer | 660 | 792 |
| Sunderland | 1,700 | 1,840 |

*Norwegian Sea*

*Faroe Islands*

Shetland Islands

Sullom Voe

• Bergen

**NORWAY¹**

• Stavanger

Scapa Flow   Orkney Islands

Invergordon

Dyce

Montrose

Leuchars

*North Sea*

Edinburgh

**DENMARK¹**

Kiel

Aldergrove

*Irish Sea*

**IRELAND²**

• Dublin

Hamburg

Wilhelmshaven

Bircham Newton

**GREAT BRITAIN**

**NETHERLANDS³**

Pembroke Dock   Carew Cheriton

London

Detling

**BELGIUM³**

**GERMANY**

Warmwell

Portsmouth

Thorney Island

Plymouth

Mount Batten

*English Channel*

**LUXEMBURG³**

Guernsey

• Paris

*ATLANTIC OCEAN*

U-26 sunk
01 Jul 1940

U-55 sunk
30 Jan 1940

HMS *Courageous*
sunk 17 Dec 1939

*Bay of Biscay*

**FRANCE**

Naval Ports

Land aircraft

Seaplane/flying boat base

Potential land-based Coastal Command air coverage

Actual air coverage by Coastal Command

1. Neutral through April 1940
2. Neutral throughout War
3. Neutral through May 1940

**OPPOSITE** STRATEGIC OVERVIEW: SEPTEMBER 1939

**Catalina:** The Consolidated Catalina, another United States import, was a twin-engine, parasol-wing flying boat, although later versions were amphibious, capable of landing on either land or water. It was slow, with a cruising speed of 125mph, but had an extremely long range (2,100nm). Extremely reliable, it could carry 4,000lb of bombs, depth charges or torpedoes. British versions were armed with seven .303 machine guns, and it could be equipped with radar. The Catalina entered service in March 1941, and 60 were operational by December that year. Catalinas were extremely effective anti-submarine aircraft. They sank one U-boat between 1939 and 1941, and would sink a total of 37 more before the war ended.

**London, Stranraer, Scapa:** The Saro London and Supermarine Stranraer and Scapa were biplane, twin-engine flying boats. All were obsolescent when the war started. The Scapa had been retired, but was brought back briefly in the first months of the war. All were slow, short-ranged and carried small bombloads. The London and Stranraer were kept only because replacement aircraft were unavailable. The Stranraer was largely retired in 1940, although the Royal Canadian Air Force flew them off the American coasts until 1943. The London was in use until June 1941, operating out of Gibraltar.

**Fleet Air Arm:** The Fleet Air Arm started the war with aircraft as inadequate as Coastal Command. Only one FAA aircraft available in 1939, the Swordfish torpedo bomber, proved a useful anti-submarine aircraft. The Blackburn Skua dive bomber, used briefly in anti-submarine warfare in September 1939, was more dangerous to its crew than to U-boats. Effective aircraft, the Grumman Martlet during this period and the Grumman Avenger torpedo bomber later in the war, were American imports.

**The Fairey Swordfish:** An open-cockpit single-engine biplane. Despite its antiquated appearance, it was deadly against U-boats in open waters, whether operating from carriers or land bases such as Gibraltar. It could carry ASV radar and 1,000lb of munitions. Swordfish sank two U-boats in 1940 and 1941, and 20 more later in the war.

Besides the Sunderland, Coastal Command's seaplane squadrons used a variety of biplane flying boats, which included the ancient Supermarine Scapa, the elderly Supermarine Stranraer (shown taking off) and the outdated Saro London. (AC)

Most Fleet Air Arm (FAA) aircraft in service when the war began were withdrawn from first-line service by the end of 1941. One exception was the Fairey Swordfish. Intended as a torpedo bomber, it proved an outstanding anti-submarine aircraft. (AC)

**The Grumman Martlet:** The export version of the United States Navy's F4F Wildcat fighter. The first Martlets acquired by the FAA came from a French order taken over after France's surrender. Although Martlets did not carry bombs, they had four .50 calibre machine guns, capable of damaging a U-boat. Used aboard escort carriers, Martlets contributed to the sinking of U-131 in December 1941, along with 26 other U-boats later in the war.

## Facilities and infrastructure

Aerial anti-U-boat infrastructure includes airfields, command structure, aircraft and munitions industries and logistics. Airfields set the scope of aerial activity. Command structure controlled deployment of effort. The aircraft industry produced the aircraft to conduct the campaign, while logistics (including flight crew training) controlled whether the resources available could be provided to fighting forces. Throughout the first two years of the Battle of the Atlantic, Coastal Command and the FAA had adequate airfields, command structure and logistics support. What they lacked was resources: aircraft, weapons and personnel.

When the war started, Coastal Command had 14 airfields assigned to active squadrons. Four were seaplane bases, sheltered anchorages allowing seaplanes to launch and land, and with facilities to arm, fuel and service seaplanes. Ten were airfields with paved runways for land-based aircraft. These bases were located to interdict enemy passage through the North Sea and English Channel, and patrol airspace immediately around Britain. One seaplane base was located on Scotland's east coast, one in the Shetlands, a third near Plymouth and a fourth in western Wales. The ten airfields were scattered in an arc starting in western Wales, running south to the English Channel, along the Channel and then near the North Sea coast to northern Scotland.

This conformed to pre-war plans that Coastal Command's primary mission was to stop enemy commercial traffic and provide reconnaissance for the Royal Navy. The Royal Air Force had other airfields and seaplane bases available, including airfields on the Shetland and Orkney Islands and aircraft and seaplane bases on the west coast of Scotland and in Northern Ireland. Squadrons could quickly redeploy if the need arose.

In several cases new airfields had to be paved before Coastal Command aircraft could operate from them. Since Bomber Command needed paved airfields for its four-engine 'heavies', Coastal Command usually came out second-best in the fight for resources. Regardless, necessary new bases, such as Aldergrove, Limavady and Nutts Corner in Northern Ireland and Stornoway in the Hebrides, were operational in 1940 and 1941.

Coastal Command also controlled two vessels, SS *Manela* and SS *Dumana*, to carry supplies, maintenance facilities and transport ground staff. They could serve as instant bases for seaplanes. When the war began, *Manela* was the base for seaplanes stationed at Sullom Voe in Shetland. Both vessels assisted Coastal Command to establish remote bases in Northern Ireland. As the war expanded, Coastal Command operated aircraft from airfields and anchorages in Iceland (Kaldadarnes and Reykjavik in 1940), Gibraltar (1940) and the West African coast (Freetown in Sierra Leone and Bathurst in Gambia, 1941).

At the war's outset, the Royal Navy possessed seven aircraft carriers, six of which were in commission, and had six more under construction. Two aircraft carriers, HMS *Ark Royal* and *Courageous*, were briefly used for anti-submarine patrols in September 1939, but after *Courageous* was sunk by a U-boat on 17 September 1939, the Royal Navy withdrew all fleet carriers from anti-submarine duties.

The FAA remained out of anti-submarine operations until June 1941, when the first escort carrier, HMS *Audacity*, entered service. Converted to an aircraft carrier from a captured liner, the ship provided an airfield that could move with a convoy. (Surprisingly, HMS *Argus*, a similar merchant conversion launched in World War I and recommissioned during World War II, was never used for convoy escort. Its characteristics, including speed, size and number of aircraft carried, were similar to most World War II escort carriers.)

Coastal Command squadrons operating out of the British Isles were organized into three Groups: 15 Group covered the Western approaches; 16 Group covered the English Channel and southern North Sea; and 18 Group held responsibility for the northern North

Some Coastal Command airfields were unpaved, as shown in this photograph. Often paved runways were not added until 1941, limiting the ability of aircraft such as the Whitley, Wellington and Liberator to operate from them. (AC)

Sea and waters around Scotland. A fourth group, 19 Group, was added in February 1941; 15 Group took the western part of 18 Group's previous area, and the northern half of its old Western Approaches area, while 19 Group assumed responsibility for the southern half of 15 Group's old region.

As Coastal Command squadrons moved overseas, Coastal Command established Air Headquarters to coordinate activities. By the end of 1941, three had been established: AHQ Iceland, AHQ Gibraltar and AHQ West Africa. Each headquarters coordinated airborne anti-submarine efforts in their region, including squadrons outside Coastal Command. In Gibraltar, this included land-based FAA squadrons.

Group headquarters were co-located with Royal Navy headquarters to facilitate communications between the two services. Co-location allowed Coastal Command to better coordinate operations and receive Royal Navy intelligence (and ultimately codebreaking intelligence from Bletchley Park) on a timely basis. Only Eighteen Group's headquarters was complete before September 1939. Communications links between the Royal Navy and Coastal Command were completed shortly after the war began.

Coastal Command began the war cooperating with the Royal Navy. As the war went on, and anti-submarine efforts fell short, closer coordination was viewed necessary. On 10 December 1940, Churchill put Coastal Command under operational control of the Royal Navy. The RAF maintained administrative control, including logistics and training.

Britain had six fleet carriers in commission in 1939. In September 1939 HMS *Ark Royal* (shown here) and HMS *Courageous* were used in anti-submarine hunter-killer groups. *Ark Royal* was hastily withdrawn from this duty after *Courageous* was sunk by a U-boat. (AC)

Coastal Command benefited from the robust logistics system of the RAF: it always had sufficient fuel and supplies for operations. The constraint was aircraft availability. It never had enough aircraft, and development of new aircraft and weapons often lagged. This was due in large part to limitations of the British aircraft industry. It was geared towards small batch production, especially for speciality aircraft. Maritime patrol and carrier aircraft, despite their importance, fell into the category of speciality aircraft. When mass production was introduced, it was used for fighters and (later) heavy bombers. Domestic production of maritime and carrier aircraft continued to follow leisurely pre-war patterns.

This situation was compounded by failures in aircraft design. The Saro Lerwick and Blackburn Botha were twin-engine patrol aircraft designed for Coastal Command to replace obsolescent designs, the Lerwick to substitute biplane flying boats and the Botha in place of the land-based Vickers Vildebeest biplane torpedo bomber. Ordered into production without a prototype, both proved failures. Both were withdrawn from active service in 1940, and are notable mainly for leaving Coastal Command short of aircraft during the war's first years.

Domestic shortfalls were made up by United States aircraft. Aware of Britain's aircraft production limitations, the Air Ministry sent the British Purchasing Commission to the United States in 1938, seeking aircraft. The Commission's first fruits were the Lockheed Hudson, but the British also purchased other important Coastal Command aircraft from the United States, including the Consolidated Hudson and Catalina, as well as the RAF's Martlets. Since the United States was neutral until December 1941, Britain effectively placed the success of its anti-U-boat campaign in the hands of a non-combatant nation.

## Weapons and tactics

Coastal Command and the Fleet Air Arm began World War II with three anti-U-boat weapons: 100lb and 250lb anti-submarine bombs and an air-droppable 450lb depth charge. Only the depth charge was capable of sinking a U-boat. In 1939, only flying boats could carry the 450lb depth charge, and the available numbers of Sunderlands (then the only non-obsolescent flying boat) and depth charges was limited. The 450lb depth charge could not be dropped at greater than 150 knots or higher than 150ft without breaking up.

# Scarecrow Patrol

Unknown to the Germans, Coastal Command aircraft were almost totally unable to destroy U-boats with aerial attacks for the first 14 months of the war. The Avro Anson was uniquely useless. It could only carry 100lb contact-fused anti-submarine bombs, which were incapable of cracking a U-boat's pressure hull with a direct hit, but had a tendency to bounce and damage the aircraft dropping them. Fortunately the Germans did not know that. Sighting a Coastal Command aircraft was enough to make a U-boat submerge, costing it mobility and reducing its ability to hunt surface ships. The Anson was in every sense a scarecrow rather than a warplane.

This plate depicts an Anson, Coastal Command's least capable but most numerous patrol aircraft, on an anti-submarine sweep over the winter sea in January 1940. The place is somewhere over the North Sea east of Scotland. The time is late afternoon. It is a clear day, but the surface of the ocean is a little hazy.

The Anson is nearing the end of a long patrol. Flying 3,000ft above the surface, it is at the end of the outbound patrol leg, just before turning for home at the far end of its patrol circuit. The tired crew missed seeing a surfaced U-boat. The U-boat was off to one side – nearly at the horizon, where it would be hard to spot anyway in the haze. The U-boat lookouts were more alert. They spotted the Anson before the Anson spotted them. It immediately dived. By the point depicted in the plate it has finished submerging. All that can be seen is a disturbed patch of water above the U-boat.

Yet despite missing its quarry, the Anson's crew has served a useful purpose. It forced the U-boat to dive. The scarecrow has indeed scared the crow.

The 100lb anti-submarine bombs were useless against submarines. They were contact weapons, requiring a hit on a surfaced vessel. Even if one did hit a U-boat, it was too weak to cause serious damage. On 3 December 1939, HMS *Snapper*, a British submarine, was struck at the base of its conning tower by a 100lb bomb dropped by a British aircraft that mistook the surfaced vessel for a German U-boat. The explosion's damage amounted to four blown light bulbs and shattered crockery. The 250lb bomb was capable of cracking the pressure hull of a U-boat – if it exploded within 6ft of the pressure hull. Unfortunately it could not be carried by the Anson, Coastal Command's primary maritime patrol aircraft in 1939 and early 1940. Both bombs proved more dangerous to the aircraft dropping them than to their intended targets. If these bombs hit the water they often bounced back into the air and then exploded. In 1939 some half a dozen anti-submarine aircraft were brought down by bombs intended for their targets.

British aircraft also lacked adequate bombsights. Only the Hudson was equipped with a bombsight, but it proved worthless at low altitudes, requiring bombing 'by eye'. Without

HMS *Snapper* took a direct hit at the base of its conning tower from two British 100lb anti-submarine bombs without serious damage. Upon returning from its patrol, during which it sank six German ships, it complained about 'friendly fire', exposing the bombs' ineffectiveness. (AC)

### AIRCRAFT ATTACK ON ENEMY SUBMARINE

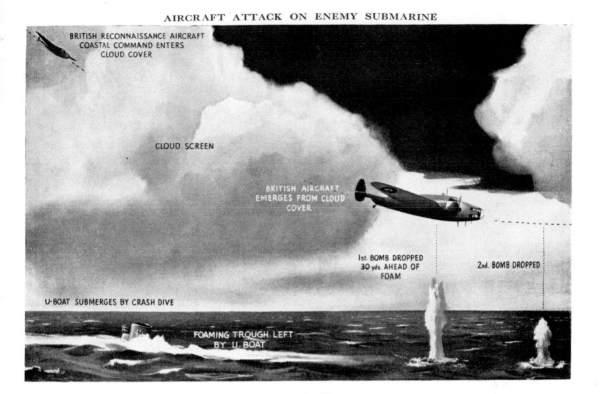

bombsights, accuracy required low-level attacks, a tactic discouraged by bombs bouncing and at night by inaccurate altimeters.

Aircraft were armed with .303 machine guns, firing a rifle-calibre bullet capable of injuring unprotected crew manning a U-boat's deck guns, but unable to penetrate either the pressure hull or the lighter metal of a U-boat's superstructure. British aircraft could suppress anti-aircraft fire from a U-boat being attacked with their machine guns, but not prevent the U-boat from successfully submerging. In 1939, apart from Sunderlands, British aircraft were better at scaring U-boats into diving than sinking them.

With experience showing the inadequacy of aerial anti-submarine weapons, Britain began developing more effective tools. For the first six months of World War II this was a low priority, since Coastal Command's primary focus was stopping German blockade runners and tracking raiding warships. But, especially after the *Snapper* incident, a more effective weapon was sought. Initial efforts focused on the Royal Navy's 250lb depth charge used by surface ships.

Tests demonstrated that unmodified 250lb depth charges would not work as air-dropped weapons. The cylinders tumbled when dropped, making accurate placement impossible. They also had a tendency to break up when dropped from too high an altitude at high speeds. Tail fins fixed the tumbling problem, allowing the depth charge to be dropped from 250ft. Torpex replaced the Amatol explosive originally filling depth charges, increasing the efficiency by 30 per cent, giving the 250lb depth charge a kill radius of 19ft. The result was a U-boat-killing weapon, which all anti-submarine aircraft (except the Anson) could use. It took until January 1941 for the 250lb depth charge to enter service, and May before it was widely used operationally.

Similar dawdling accompanied the introduction of radar. Britain tested its first airborne Air to Surface Vessel (ASV) radar in 1937, but it took until January 1940 for Coastal Command to begin operational use of ASV. Mk I radars could locate a convoy. After radar

This drawing shows the mode of attack used prior to July 1941, when Operation *Research* modified tactics. Note how the aircraft lines up on the U-boat. Additionally, 250lb anti-submarine bombs were useless once the U-boat submerged. (AC)

October 1939

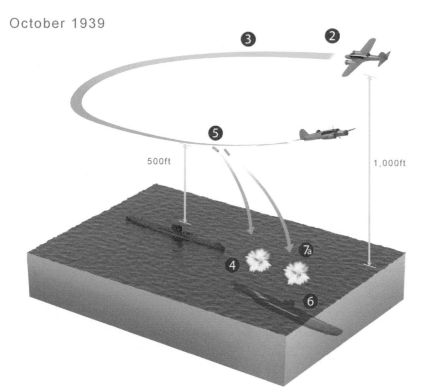

500ft

1,000ft

October 1941

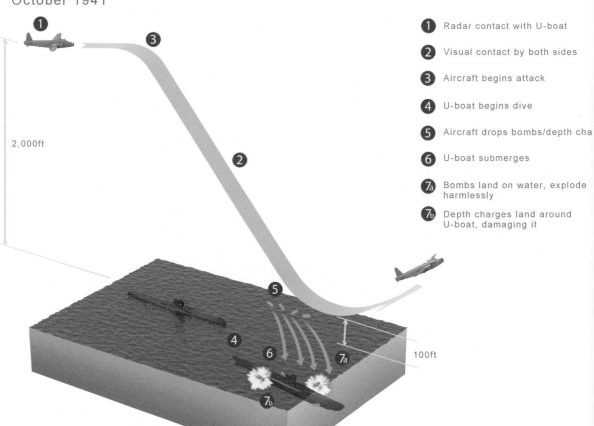

2,000ft

100ft

1  Radar contact with U-boat

2  Visual contact by both sides

3  Aircraft begins attack

4  U-boat begins dive

5  Aircraft drops bombs/depth cha

6  U-boat submerges

7a  Bombs land on water, explode harmlessly

7b  Depth charges land around U-boat, damaging it

# OPPOSITE OPERATIONAL RESEARCH BEARS FRUIT, OCTOBER 1939–OCTOBER 1941

reflectors were installed at Coastal Command bases, radar-equipped patrolling aircraft also used radar as navigation aids in bad weather.

Radar's use against submarines was limited. Mark I radars could spot a fully surfaced submarine oriented broadside-on to the set at a maximum range of only 3nm when the aircraft was at 1,000ft and 6 miles at 6,000ft. It was incapable of spotting a periscope or even a conning tower. Performance improved with a new antenna configuration using two receivers with a sideways-looking antenna array. Only 50 aircraft were fitted with Mark I radar by the end of 1940.

Mark II radar was better. It had a maximum range of 36 miles and was more reliable. Developed in early 1940, it became operational in July that year. Coastal Command installed several thousand Mk II radar sets on Hudsons, Sunderlands, Wellingtons, Whitleys and Liberators, and the FAA also equipped Swordfish with these units. The first successful interception of a U-boat by the Mk II occurred in November 1941, when a Whitley attacked and damaged U-71 as the U-boat transited the Bay of Biscay. By mid-1941, Mk II radars had increased U-boat interceptions in the Bay by 20 per cent.

The weakness of all early radars was that they had a minimum range of between ¼ mile and 1 mile. As an aircraft approached the submarine, ground clutter – reflection of waves – hid the U-boat. This mattered little in a daytime attack, as the U-boat could be targeted visually at that range. At night, however, especially on moonless nights with a slow-moving U-boat producing no tell-tale wake, it rendered the U-boat invisible.

Aerial flares overcame the limitations of darkness when deployed properly, which was a difficult task. The answer was the Leigh light: an aimable forward-pointing spotlight mounted on patrol aircraft. It illuminated the target at ranges the radars lost lock. However, the installation was large and heavy, using a 20in or 24in spotlight, with a dedicated generator. Only large multi-engine aircraft could carry it. The Hudson could not.

Wing Commander Humphrey de Verd Leigh developed the light system in late 1940, testing a prototype in March 1941 aboard a Wellington modified for anti-mine operations. Only then did he inform his Coastal Command superiors. Coastal Command's chief, Frederick Bowhill, was enthusiastic. To save time, the Air Ministry wanted to use an already-operational airborne spotlight, the Turbinelight. Developed to intercept aircraft, trials revealed Turbinelight inadequately illuminated U-boats. The Air Ministry revisited the Leigh light, but this delayed its introduction until 1942.

It took almost as long to develop effective tactics as it did effective weapons. On 25 July 1941, Coastal Command issued tactical instructions for attacks on U-boats. The average ASV contact range was 9 miles, and the typical visual sighting range was 6 miles for both aircraft and submarines. U-boats could dive in 25 seconds, which meant a U-boat would typically be submerged when aircraft arrived.

The tactical instructions worked within these constraints. Attacks were to be made by the shortest path at the maximum speed. Depth charges were the preferred weapon, as bombs were ineffective once the boat submerged. Depth charges were to be set to explode at a 50ft depth, with a 60ft spacing between depth charges. If possible, all depth charges carried should be dropped on the first attack. When possible, depth charges should be dropped from a 100ft altitude.

Experience modified this doctrine: 100ft spacing proved more effective than 60ft. The ideal depth setting for depth charges was 25–32ft, but pistols capable of triggering at that depth were not yet available. Operational effectiveness, virtually nil prior to these instructions, jumped dramatically. By November 1941, Coastal Command was deadly.

# DEFENDERS' CAPABILITIES
## Wolves and Condors

A Type IIB U-boat heading out on a war patrol. Type II submarines displaced 250 tons surfaced. Considered coastal submarines, over half of Germany's commissioned U-boats on 1 September 1939 were Type IIs. (AC)

A U-boat is an offensive weapon, designed to seek out and destroy enemy ships. In most histories of the Battle of the Atlantic, the submarines are the attacker, while the cargo ships and their escorts are defending. Even when surface warships are hunting submarines, their best tactics are defensive: stick near a convoy. You are more likely to run across a U-boat there than wandering randomly around the ocean. Then you can counterpunch when the U-boats appear.

When aircraft become involved, the dynamic reverses. A U-boat is hard to see from sea level, but surfaced U-boats, or those just below the surface, leave a tell-tale wake that is easier to spot from the air than the aircraft is to spot from a U-boat. U-boats carried a light anti-aircraft battery, making it difficult to effectively attack aircraft. A U-boat's best defence is to submerge, but once underwater they cannot attack aircraft. Patrolling aircraft are no more likely to spot a U-boat in any particular spot in open ocean than are patrolling surface vessels. However aircraft can cover so much more area during one patrol that their odds of spotting at least one surfaced U-boat are pretty good. Moreover, U-boats needed to stay surfaced at least half the time.

U-boats play cats to the surface ships' mice, but cats are vulnerable to eagles. Maritime patrol aircraft are intelligent eagles, willing to forgo rodents to attack cats – or enemy condors also seeking surface ship mice.

### The U-boat and Fw 200

The two main weapons Germany used against ships during the Battle of the Atlantic between September 1939 and December 1941 were the U-boat and Fw 200 Condor bomber. Surface raiders – conventional warships and disguised raiders – played only minor roles in creating shipping losses. British aerial efforts therefore concentrated on seeking out and destroying U-boats, but did not neglect the Condor.

The Germans used three major types of U-boats in the Battle of the Atlantic between 1939 and 1941: Type II (in four variants), Type VII and Type IX. Additionally, they had several miscellaneous types: the Type IA, UA – a submarine built for Turkey in Germany – and the Type XB. (The Type IA was similar to Type IX and the UA similar to Type VII. Type XB was a large minelaying submarine, just entering service in late 1941, which did not see combat service until 1942.) Italy also sent 32 submarines into the Atlantic between entering the war in June 1940 and December 1941. Until the development of the snorkel, U-boats and submarines principally operated on the surface, submerging only to avoid enemy warships and aircraft. They can be thought of as torpedo boats that submerged only when necessary.

**Type IIA, IIB, IIC and IID**: The Type II U-boat was the smallest seagoing submarine used by the Kriegsmarine. They were classed as 250-ton vessels based on their surfaced displacement, although they actually varied between 380 and 460 tons displacement. The Type IIA was based upon a design based on *Vesikko*, a submarine launched in 1933, built in Finland by Germans.

Fifty Type II U-boats were built in the four design variants. All had three 21in torpedo tubes forward, and carried two spare torpedoes for a total of five. When the war started they were also armed with one 20mm anti-aircraft gun that could be used against aircraft or ships. Type IIs had a top surface speed of 12–13 knots and a surface cruising speed of 8 knots. The primary difference between the variants was range, which increased from 1,600nm for the IIA to 5,600nm for the IID.

Intended as a coastal boat, and handicapped by its small load of torpedoes, the Type IIs were primarily used in the North Sea and Baltic Sea in 1939 and 1940. (Three Type IICs conducted combat patrols out of Lorient in 1940.) By 1941 all had been retired to training flotillas.

**Type VIIA, VIIB and VIIC**: The Type VII was classified as a 750-ton vessel, although the three types varied from 745 to 757 tons. All had five 21in torpedo tubes (four forward, one aft), with the VIIA carrying 11 torpedoes and the VIIB and VIIC 14 torpedoes. The top speed varied between 17 and 17.7 knots while surfaced, with a surface cruising speed of 10 knots. Between 1939 and 1941, Type VII boats were typically equipped with one 88mm deck gun and one light anti-aircraft gun. As with the Type II U-boats, the difference between the

Nearly 600 of the 500-ton Type VII U-boats were built. The Type VIIC was the most numerous, with 568 commissioned. The U-boat pictured is a Type VIIB, believed to be U-47, commanded by Gunter Prien. (USNHHC)

A 1,000-ton design, the Type IX submarine, measured by tonnage sunk per U-boat, was the most successful. Eight of the top ten U-boats in terms of tonnage and number of ships sunk were various Type IX designs. (AC)

three classes was range. The VIIA's range was 6,200nm. Saddle tanks on the VIIBs increased that to 8,700nm, and the VIIC (the most common variant) could go 8,500nm.

The Type VII was intended for Atlantic operations, and was the most numerous type used in the Battle of the Atlantic. The Type VII was popular with its crews. It was agile surfaced, and dived quickly. They were particularly useful during the first two years of the war, when operating in the eastern Atlantic, relatively close to French bases.

Ten Type VIIA boats were built, all prior to the war. The Type VIIBs were built between 1936 and 1940, and in all 50 were built. Type VIIC, the workhorse of the U-boats, started seeing service in 1940. By the war's end, 568 were commissioned, but only 154 had entered service by the end of 1941. Forty-nine of those were still completing training prior to conducting their first combat patrol.

**Type IX, IXB and IXC**: The Type IXs were large, ocean-going U-boats, intended for extended operations. There were three variants, with displacements ranging from 1,050 and 1,120 tons. The Type IXs had six torpedo tubes (four forward, two aft) and carried 22 21in torpedoes (with ten externally in deck containers). It was armed with a 105mm deck gun, and in 1939–40 with a light anti-aircraft gun. It had a surface cruising speed of 10 knots, and a maximum surface speed of 18.2 knots. The boat was capable of extremely long range, from 10,500 miles for the Type IX up to 13,500 miles for the Type IXC.

Eight Type IXs were built, all pre-war, along with 14 IXBs between 1937 and 1940 and 54 IXCs, of which 41 were in commission before 1941 ended. They were less popular than the Type VII boats as they took longer to submerge, and were less agile on the surface. However, the most successful patrols of the war were conducted by Type IXBs.

**Fw 200**: The Fw 200 Condor became an important part of the Battle of the Atlantic after France surrendered in June 1940. The Fw 200 was originally built as a transatlantic airliner. It was hastily converted to a long-range maritime patrol aircraft by attaching a bomb bay beneath the fuselage and adding machine guns and cannon for both anti-shipping and air-to-air defence. During the summer and autumn of 1940, convoys sailing from Britain dispersed at 19 degrees west longitude. The ships, generally unarmed, then sailed independently to North America. Long-range Condors could reach 24 degrees west, attacking unprotected ships with impunity. Condors could also trail convoys beyond anti-aircraft range, vectoring U-boats.

However, the Condor was structurally weak and virtually helpless against fighters (or even Coastal Command patrol bombers), but during the first six months it was used, it faced no opposition and became the terror of the Atlantic.

The main factor limiting German ambitions in the Battle of the Atlantic was shortages of both U-boats and Condors. There were simply never enough. Germany had 56 U-boats when World War II began, including vessels used only for training. Pre-war plans called for 118 U-boats by 1942, but increasing U-boat numbers to anywhere near such a level in 1939 and 1940 was difficult. Even by the end of 1941, only 80 or so U-boats were available for combat operations in the Atlantic, and some were being transferred to the Mediterranean. Similarly, the Condors on maritime patrol never numbered higher than a few dozen during the critical period from September 1940 to July 1941.

## Facilities and infrastructure

For Germany in the Battle of the Atlantic, geography was crucial to its destiny. Its ability to attack Britain's commerce was constrained or facilitated by its available bases.

When the war began, Germany had only three bases for U-boats: Kiel, Hamburg and Wilhelmshaven. Hamburg and Kiel were also administrative centres. These bases were located on Germany's north coast, with Kiel on the Baltic coast in Schleswig-Holstein, while Hamburg and Wilhelmshaven were on the North Sea. To reach Atlantic shipping, U-boats had to run the narrow, well-guarded English Channel, or cross the North Sea and sail around Scotland.

Going between the Shetlands and Norway to exit the North Sea added 600nm to the trip to reach Britain's Western Approaches. Once the English Channel was closed, a trip to reach the Channel Approaches around Britain (viable until the fall of France in June 1940) was 1,300nm. This limited the time a U-boat could spend on what were then the most productive Atlantic hunting grounds.

One motivation for invading Norway was escaping this geographic trap. With the rapid conquest of Norway, U-boats could use Kristiansand, Stavanger and Bergen for refuelling as early as late April 1940, increasing their operational radius by 300nm. U-boats still had to

The FW 200 Condor was a bomber version of the four-engine Kurier airliner. Although an improvised design, since it virtually always attacked unarmed ships steaming individually, its weaknesses were hidden. (AC)

## OPPOSITE STRATEGIC OVERVIEW: OCTOBER 1940

return to Germany for supplies and munitions until late summer that year, but they could make the voyage within the umbrella of German fighter cover. The Norwegian occupation also broke the Scotland–Norway barrier maintained by Britain. Norway-based German fighters thereafter made it too dangerous for British seaplanes (or Hudsons) to patrol between the Shetlands and Norway. The Germans began building U-boat base facilities at Trondheim and Bergen that autumn, but most were not completed until 1942.

They largely went unfinished because the fall of France made Norwegian bases superfluous. The peace settlement permitted Germany to occupy France's Channel and Atlantic coasts. The U-boats thereby gained new ports right on Britain's doorstep, including Brest, the main harbour of France's Atlantic fleet, which reopened under German management. Germany also set up U-boat bases at Lorient, St Nazaire, La Pallice/ La Rochelle and Bordeaux.

These bases outflanked Britain's 1939–40 U-boat barriers and cut off the Channel Approaches until 1944. All supplies coming to Britain had to loop north of Ireland through the North Channel. Convoys sailing between Britain and Africa (which were always of high value) were literally just a day away for U-boats based on the French Atlantic coast.

These four U-boats belong to 7. Flotille (7th Flotilla), photographed in harbour at Kiel between February and August 1939. When World War II started, a major constraint on U-boat operations were the locations of their bases, the German ports of Wilhelmshaven, Hamburg and Kiel. (AC)

U-boats began operating out of French ports in July 1940, when U-30 stopped at Lorient to refuel and resupply. U-boats began operating out of Brest in August that year and St Nazaire, La Pallice and Bordeaux in September. Additionally, three Italian submarines arrived at Bordeaux that September, the first of 32 Italian submarines to join the Battle of the Atlantic. Italian submarines operated out of Bordeaux, with La Pallice as a backup.

Germany built extensive facilities in all of its new bases, especially the French ports. They soon transferred flotilla headquarters from Germany to France. The 2nd Flotilla was first to move, relocating from Kiel to Lorient in July 1940. Over the rest of 1940, the 1st Flotilla

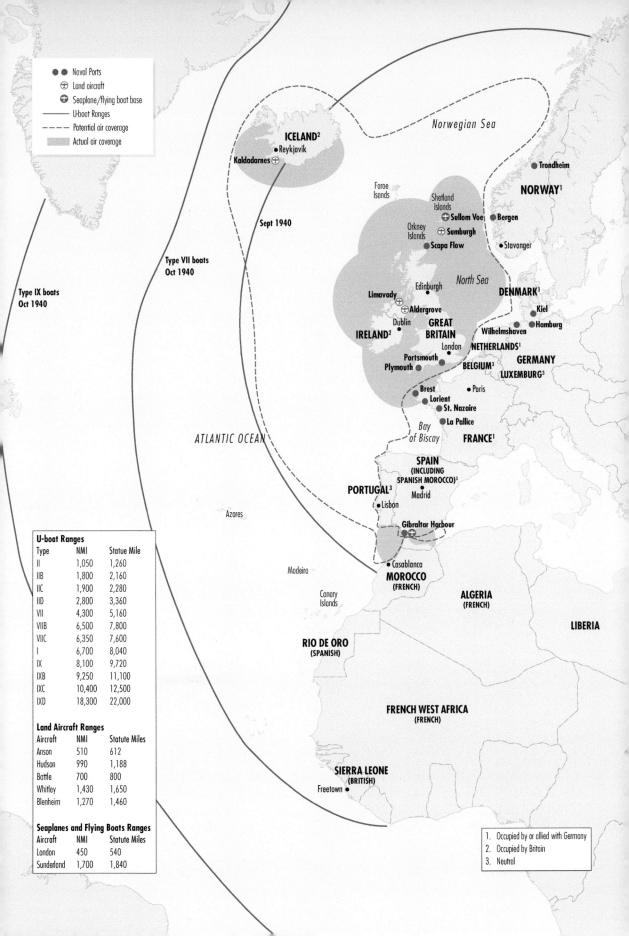

**Legend:**
- ● ● Naval Ports
- ⊕ Land aircraft
- ✈ Seaplane/flying boat base
- —— U-boat Ranges
- ---- Potential air coverage
- ▨ Actual air coverage

Norwegian Sea

ICELAND[2]
• Reykjavik
Kaldadarnes ✈

Sept 1940

Type VII boats
Oct 1940

Type IX boats
Oct 1940

Faroe Islands

Shetland Islands
✈ Sullom Voe
Orkney Islands
⊕ Sumburgh
• Scapa Flow

NORWAY[1]
• Trondheim
• Bergen
• Stavanger

North Sea

Limavady
⊕ Aldergrove
Edinburgh

DENMARK[1]
• Kiel
• Hamburg

Dublin
IRELAND[2]

GREAT BRITAIN
London
Portsmouth
Plymouth

Wilhelmshaven
NETHERLANDS[1]
BELGIUM[3]
GERMANY
LUXEMBURG[3]

• Brest
• Lorient
• St. Nazaire
• La Pallice

• Paris

FRANCE[1]

Bay of Biscay

ATLANTIC OCEAN

Azores

SPAIN
(INCLUDING SPANISH MOROCCO)[3]

PORTUGAL[3]
• Madrid
• Lisbon

Gibraltar Harbour

Madeira

• Casablanca
MOROCCO (FRENCH)

ALGERIA (FRENCH)

LIBERIA

Canary Islands

RIO DE ORO (SPANISH)

FRENCH WEST AFRICA (FRENCH)

SIERRA LEONE (BRITISH)
Freetown •

**U-boat Ranges**

| Type | NMI | Statue Mile |
|------|------|-------------|
| II | 1,050 | 1,260 |
| IIB | 1,800 | 2,160 |
| IIC | 1,900 | 2,280 |
| IID | 2,800 | 3,360 |
| VII | 4,300 | 5,160 |
| VIIB | 6,500 | 7,800 |
| VIIC | 6,350 | 7,600 |
| I | 6,700 | 8,040 |
| IX | 8,100 | 9,720 |
| IXB | 9,250 | 11,100 |
| IXC | 10,400 | 12,500 |
| IXD | 18,300 | 22,000 |

**Land Aircraft Ranges**

| Aircraft | NMI | Statute Miles |
|----------|------|---------------|
| Anson | 510 | 612 |
| Hudson | 990 | 1,188 |
| Battle | 700 | 800 |
| Whitley | 1,430 | 1,650 |
| Blenheim | 1,270 | 1,460 |

**Seaplanes and Flying Boats Ranges**

| Aircraft | NMI | Statute Miles |
|----------|------|---------------|
| London | 450 | 540 |
| Sunderland | 1,700 | 1,840 |

1. Occupied by or allied with Germany
2. Occupied by Britain
3. Neutral

In late 1940 Germany began building reinforced-concrete berths to shelter their U-boats in port. Virtually bomb-proof when completed, these bunkers would have been easily destroyed through bombing during construction, due to the caissons needed for their foundations. (USNHHC)

and 9th Flotilla moved to Brest, the 3rd to La Pallice and the 7th to St Nazaire. Dönitz also moved U-boat headquarters to France, first to Paris in September and then to Lorient in November 1940.

To protect the U-boats in harbour, an enormous shelter-building project began in 1940. These were massive, reinforced concrete bunkers, several hundred yards wide and long, protected by concrete roofs as much as 6 yards thick. Impervious to conventional bombs, these submarine pens were erected in German, Norwegian and French ports. The French bunkers were started and completed first. Each French port had at least one pen by the end of 1941. Those protecting German-based U-boats were started soon after, with the Norwegian submarine pens completed last. Similar shelters were erected at shipyards in Germany manufacturing U-boats.

These pens meant U-boats could remain in port unmolested and receive necessary repairs and maintenance without risk of damage. Bombing could delay manufacturing, but only by disrupting supplies before they reached the yards. Once materials were under shelter, they were virtually impossible to destroy. Surprisingly, the British never attempted to bomb these shelters while they were under construction and vulnerable to attack. Instead, the first raids were mounted in 1942, beyond the scope of this book and after the pens were completed.

Nineteen shipyards built U-boats for the Kriegsmarine. The most important U-boat construction centres were Hamburg (384 U-boats delivered and commissioned), Kiel (241 U-boats), Bremen (262 U-boats) and Danzig (136 U-boats). These four cities produced

89 per cent of the U-boats commissioned by the Kriegsmarine. Most construction occurred after 1941. Sixty-three U-boats were built prior to World War II, 50 in 1940 and 199 completed in 1941.

AG Weser in Bremen and Deutsche Werke AG and F. Krupp Germaniawerft AG in Kiel had completed U-boats before World War II started. The rest, including the largest shipyard, Blohm & Voss in Hamburg, did not start building U-boats until immediately before or after the war started. This delayed the build-up of U-boats whilst the infrastructure to build them was constructed.

Condors operated from bases in Norway and France. While Norwegian bases opened first, convoy patterns meant French bases were closer to the merchant ships. The main airfield for anti-shipping Condors was Mérignac at Bordeaux, although they also flew from bases at Brest. One infrastructure weakness was the inability of the Luftwaffe and Kriegsmarine to cooperate due to inter-service rivalry. Sightings by Condors often went unreported to the Kriegsmarine, or were delayed long enough to become useless.

## Weapons and tactics

The U-boat was an offensive weapon fighting defensively against aircraft. Its offensive weapons played as important a role in understanding what made it vulnerable to aircraft as its defensive capabilities played in defending against aircraft. Additionally, new U-boat tactics were a way to overcome its weaknesses. This was also true of the Fw 200.

The U-boat's main weapon was the 21in torpedo. Two types were in service at the start of World War II: the G7s T1 compressed air torpedo and the G7e T2 electrically powered torpedo. Both carried a 280kg (617lb) Hexanite-filled warhead. Hexanite, developed before World War I, was more powerful than TNT. A single warhead had three times the power of a World War I-era torpedo warhead. A single hit was thus capable of sinking most merchant ships.

Both could be fitted with either a contact trigger, which detonated upon striking a ship, or a magnetic trigger, set off by a ship's magnetic field. The magnetic fuse was designed to run under a ship and explode beneath it, breaking the ship's back. Many nations developed magnetic triggers before World War II, and all experienced similar problems with them: they frequently failed to detonate properly, exploding prematurely or not at all. The problem was exacerbated in northern latitudes. Germany therefore abandoned magnetic triggers in 1940.

The compressed air torpedoes had a range of 8,000 metres when set for 40 knots, or 14,000 metres at 30 knots. Their main drawback was that these torpedoes left a visible surface trail of bubbles as they travelled, potentially warning targets of their approach. The electric torpedoes could reach 5,000m at their 30-knot setting, if preheated. They could also be assembled with fewer man-hours.

Type II boats carried only five torpedoes; the Type VII boats had 14 and the Type IXs up to 22. Since the ocean-going boats carried only four torpedo tubes forward (and one or two aft), no more than four torpedoes could be fired with one targeting solution, and a maximum of six (expending torpedoes loaded in both bow and stern tubes) at one time. A U-boat had few torpedoes, and to have even a chance of a hit it had to be close – within 3 nautical miles – of its target. To have a good chance to score a hit, it had to be even closer.

In addition to torpedoes, the submarines of 1939–41 carried an anti-aircraft gun, while the larger U-boats had a deck gun; 88mm for the Type VIIs and 105mm for Type IAs and Type IXs. The main defence against aircraft was the single 20mm gun mounted on the conning tower. While the 88mm had anti-aircraft capabilities, it was better against aircraft flying at constant altitudes and course. Using it against an aircraft flying straight at the U-boat was challenging, as the shell had to be fused to explode at a specific range. Knocking down an aircraft required luck: either a low-odds direct hit or a lucky guess at the aircraft's range when the gun was fired.

The U-boat's best defence against aircraft was invisibility. Until reliable radar was installed on anti-submarine aircraft, night hid a surfaced U-boat from searching aircraft, except under unusual circumstances. Regardless of time of day, a U-boat became invisible once it dived. While ships could track submerged U-boats with ASDIC, until after the end of 1941 aircraft had no means of detecting a submerged U-boat.

All aircraft could do was drop depth charges near where the U-boat was last spotted. Since (unknown to the Germans) the only aircraft capable of carrying air-droppable depth charges until the 250lb depth charge was introduced were Sunderlands, even a few feet of

The U-boat's main weapon was the torpedo. Both the G7s T1 compressed air and G7e T2 electrically powered torpedo had ranges in excess of ASDIC, meaning a U-boat could strike a convoy well outside the detection range of its escorts. (USNHHC)

water between the U-boat and the surface made it invulnerable to air attack. Even after air-droppable depth charges became available, not until after 1941 were fuses obtainable to reliably detonate depth charges at the optimal 25ft setting.

There were two issues resulting from submerging. One was that the U-boat became detectable by nearby ASDIC-equipped warships. Even in daylight, a surfaced U-boat, hull-down so only the conning tower was above the surface, was virtually invisible to a surface warship. Submerged, it appeared on ASDIC. Warships in combination with aircraft could be deadly. Virtually all U-boat kills involving aircraft in 1939–41 involved a combination of surface warships and aircraft. Either the aircraft forced the U-boat to submerge, with a warship sinking it, or the warship damaged a U-boat's ability to submerge and the aircraft finished it off.

The second issue was that U-boats needed to remain surfaced for much of a day, and not just to recharge batteries and replace stale air. A submerged U-boat was virtually blind, losing most of its capability for reconnaissance. A convoy could be spotted over the horizon by the smoke it produced, but only from the deck. A submerged U-boat was also virtually immobile. Its maximum submerged speed was one-third its surface speed, and an hour or two at maximum speed exhausted the batteries running the U-boat's electric motors.

A U-boat could not communicate submerged, and had to surface to use its radio. U-boats were expected to use radio to report all convoy sightings, and report them before attacking the convoy. From his headquarters, Dönitz would correlate reports and order nearby U-boats towards the convoy. In June 1940, Dönitz began launching multi-U-boat (wolf-pack) attacks on convoys coordinated by radio.

Finally, Dönitz intended U-boats to make surface attacks on convoys. Surfaced at night, U-boats were virtually invisible. At or even above convoy speeds their diesels could not be heard over the noise of the convoy's ships. They could not be detected on ASDIC. Dönitz's best U-boat aces would slip into a convoy when the night was moonless, attack the convoy from the inside and then submerge, their escape masked from ASDIC by noise generated by the ships that were struck and sinking. Not until radar – surface and ASV – stripped U-boats of their nocturnal invisibility were new tactics needed. That occurred only as 1941 closed.

In World War I, a U-boat's deck gun was its primary weapon. By World War II, U-boats still had them, but they were generally used to finish off crippled and abandoned vessels that a torpedo had failed to sink. (AC)

# Order of Battle

## Allies
## 3 September 1939
## Coastal Command

| 15 Group – HQ Plymouth | | |
|---|---|---|
| Squadron | Base | Aircraft |
| 204 | Mount Batten | Sunderland |
| 210 | Pembroke Dock | Sunderland |
| 228 | Pembroke Dock | Sunderland |
| 217 | Warmwell, Carew Cheriton | Anson |
| 502 (RAuxAF) | Aldergrove | Anson |

| 16 Group – HQ Chatham | | |
|---|---|---|
| Squadron | Base | Aircraft |
| 42 | Bircham Newton | Vildebeest |
| 206 | Bircham Newton | Anson |
| 22 | Thorney Island | Vildebeest |
| 48 | Thorney Island, Detling, Guernsey | Anson |
| 500 (RAuxAF) | Detling | Anson |

| 18 Group – HQ Pitreavie Castle, Rosyth | | |
|---|---|---|
| Squadron | Base | Aircraft |
| 201 | Sullom Voe (SS Manela) | London |
| 209 | Invergordon | Stranraer |
| 240 | Invergordon | London |
| 220 | Thornaby | Anson |
| 608 (RAuxAF) | Thornaby | Anson |
| 224 | Leuchars | Hudson |
| 233 | Leuchars | Anson |
| 269 | Montrose | Anson |
| 612 (RAuxAF) | Dyce | Anson |

## Royal Navy
(Aircraft carriers and complement)
HMS *Eagle* – 18 Swordfish (813, 824 Squadrons)
HMS *Hermes* – 9 Swordfish (814 Squadron)
HMS *Furious* – 18 Swordfish (767 Squadron), 8 Skuas (769 Squadron), 4 Rocs (769 Squadron)
HMS *Courageous* – 24 Swordfish (811, 822 Squadrons)
HMS *Glorious* – 36 Swordfish (812, 823, 825 Squadrons), 12 Sea Gladiators (802 Squadron)
HMS *Ark Royal* – 42 Swordfish (810, 820, 818, 821 Squadrons), 18 Skuas (800, 803 Squadrons)

## 16 November 1941
## Coastal Command

| 15 Group – HQ Liverpool | | |
|---|---|---|
| Squadron | Base | Aircraft |
| 53 | Limavady | Hudson |
| 120 | Nutts Corner | Liberator |
| 143 | Aldergrove | Blenheim IV |
| 201 | Lough Erne | Sunderland |
| 206 | Aldergrove | Hudson |
| 210 | Oban | Catalina |
| 228 | Stranraer | Sunderland |
| 240 | Lough Erne | Catalina |

| 16 Group – HQ Chatham | | |
|---|---|---|
| Squadron | Base | Aircraft |
| 22 | Thorney Island | Beaufort |
| 59 | North Coates | Hudson |
| 217 | Thorney Island | Beaufort |
| 224 | Limavady | Hudson |
| 248 | Bircham Newton | Beaufighter |
| 279 | Bircham Newton | Hudson |
| 407 (RCAF) | North Coates | Hudson |
| 415 (RCAF) | Thorney Island | Hampton/Beaufort |
| 500 (RAuxAF) | Bircham Newton | Hudson |
| 502 (RAuxAF) | Bircham Newton | Whitley |

| 18 Group – HQ Pitreavie Castle, Rosyth | | |
|---|---|---|
| Squadron | Base | Aircraft |
| 42 | Leuchars | Beaufort |
| 48 | Wick | Hudson |
| 220 | Wick | Fortress |
| 235 | Dyce | Blenheim IVf |
| 320 (Neth) | Leuchars | Hudson |
| 404 (RCAF) | Sumburgh | Blenheim IV |
| 413 (RCAF) | Sullom Voe | Catalina |
| 489 (RNZAF) | Leuchars | Beaufort |
| 608 (RAuxAF) | Wick | Hudson |

| 19 Group – HQ Plymouth | | |
|---|---|---|
| Squadron | Base | Aircraft |
| 22 (detachment) | St Eval | Beaufort |
| 86 | St Eval | Beaufort |
| 209 | Pembroke Dock | Catalina |
| 217 | St Eval | Beaufort |
| 233 | St Eval | Hudson |
| 254 | Carew Cheriton | Blenheim IV |
| 502 (detachment) | St Eval | Whitley |
| 10 RAAF | Mount Batten | Sunderland |
| 1017 Flt | Chivenor | Wellington |

| AHQ Gibraltar | | |
|---|---|---|
| Squadron | Base | Aircraft |
| 202 | Gibraltar | Sunderland/ Catalina |
| 812 (FAA) | Gibraltar | Swordfish |
| 813 (FAA) | Gibraltar | Swordfish |
| 816 (FAA) | Gibraltar | Swordfish |

| AHQ Iceland | | |
|---|---|---|
| Squadron | Base | Aircraft |
| 269 | Kaldadarnes | Hudson |
| 330 (Nwg) | Reykjavik | Northrop N3P-B |
| 612 (RAuxAF) | Reykjavik | Whitley |
| VP-73 (USN) | Reykjavik | Catalina |
| VP-74 (USN) | Reykjavik | Marina |

| AHQ West Africa | | |
|---|---|---|
| Squadron | Base | Aircraft |
| 95 | Freetown, Sierra Leone | Sunderland |
| 200 | Banjul, Gambia | Hudson |
| 204 | Banjul, Gambia | Sunderland |

## Royal Navy
(only aircraft carriers involved in ASW activity)
HMS *Audacity* – 802 squadron (Martlets)

## Axis
### 3 September 1939
### 1. Unterseebootsflottille 'Weddigen' (Kiel)
IIB: U-7*, U-9*, U-13*, U-15*, U-17*, U-18+, U-19*, U-23*
IIC: U-57+, U-58*

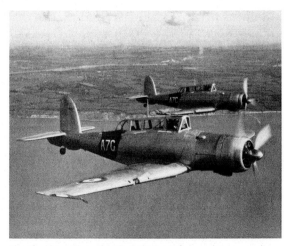

The Blackburn Skua, the Fleet Air Arm's first modern monoplane, was obsolescent by 1939. FAA aircraft's performance lagged behind other nations' carrier aircraft, due in large part to the Air Ministry's disinterest in developing naval aircraft. (AC)

### 2. Unterseebootsflottille 'Wegener' (Wilhelmshaven)
VIIA: U-32+, U-33*, U-34*, U-35+, U-36
### 3. Unterseebootsflottille 'Lohs' (Kiel)
IIB: U-12*, U-14+, U-16*, U-20*, U-21*, U-22, U-24*
### 5. Unterseebootsflottille (Kiel)
IA: U-25, U-26*
VIIA: U-27*, U-28*, U-29*, U-30*, U-31+
### 6. Unterseebootsflottille 'Hundius' (Kiel)
IX: U-37*, U-38*, U-39*, U-40*, U-41*
### 7. Unterseebootsflottille 'Wegener' (Kiel)
VIIB: U-45*, U46*, U-47*, U-48*, U-51*, U-52*, U-53*
### U-Bootschulflottille (Kiel)
IIA: U-1, U-2, U-3, U-4, U-5, U-6
IIB: U-8, U-10, U-11
### Training
IIC: U-56, U-59, U-60, U-61
IX: U-42, U-43, U-49
* At sea, war patrol North Sea/North Atlantic
+ At sea, war patrol, Baltic Sea
### 16 November 1941
### 1. Unterseebootsflottille (Brest)
**VIIB**: U-83, U-84
**VIIC**: U-201, U-202, U-203, U-208, U-372, U-374, U-557, U-558, U-561, U-562, U-563, U-564, U-565, U-566, U-574, U-654
### 2. Unterseebootsflottille (Lorient)
**IX**: U-38, U-43
**IXB**: U-103, U-105, U-106, U-107, U-108, U-109, U-123, U-124
**IXC**: U-66, U-67, U-68, U-125, U-126, U-127, U-129, U-131, U-502
**Saldiray class** (ex-Turkish): U-A
### 3. Unterseebootsflottille (La Pallice/ La Rochelle)
**VIIB**: U-85
**VIIC**: U-82, U-134, U-206, U-332, U-373, U-375, U-402, U-431, U-432, U-433, U-451, U-568, U-569, U-571, U-572, U-573, U-652, U-752
### 7. Unterseebootsflottille (St Nazaire)
**VIIB**: U-101
**VIIC**: U-69, U-71, U-73, U-74, U-77, U-93, U-94, U-95, U-96, U-98, U-133, U-403, U-434, U-453, U-454, U-552, U-553, U-567, U-575, U-576, U-577, U-578, U-756
### 9. Unterseebootsflottille (Brest)
(Formed in October 1941 – no boats yet assigned)
**School Flotillas** (U-boats permanently assigned to training)
### 21. Ausbildungsflottille (Pillau)
**IIA**: U-2, U-3, U-4, U-5, U-6
**IIB**: U-7, U-9, U-10, U-20, U-21, U-23, U-24, U-120, U-121

Heinkel floatplanes escort U-28 out of Kiel harbour in a pre-war photograph. (AC)

**IIC**: U-60, U-61, U-62
**IID**: U-141, U-148, U-151, U-152
**VIIC**: U-72
**22. Ausbildungsflottille (Gotenhafen)**
**IIB**: U-8, U-11, U-14, U-17, U-18, U-19
**IIC**: U-56, U-57, U-58, U-59
**IID**: U-137, U-139, U-140, U-142, U-143, U-144, U-146, U-149, U-150
**VIIA**: U-28
**VIIB**: U-78
**24. Ausbildungsflottille (Memel)**
**VIIA**: U-29, U-30
**VIIC**: U-554, U-555, U-560
**26. Ausbildungsflottille (Pillau)**
**VIIB**: U-46, U-48, U-52
**VIIC**: U-80
**IX**: U-37
**Undergoing Training** (U-boats completing training prior to assignment to combat flotillas)
**VIIB**: U-87
**VIIC**: U-88, U-135, U-136, U-209, U-251, U-252, U-253, U-254, U-333, U-334, U-352, U-355, U-376,

U-377, U-378, U-404, U-405, U-406, U-435, U-436, U-437, U-455, U-456, U-457, U-459, U-581, U-582, U-584, U-585, U-586, U-587, U-588, U-589, U-591, U-592, U-593, U-594, U-595, U-596, U-653,U-655, U-656, U-657, U-658, U-701, U-702, U-703, U-753, U-754, U-755
**VIID**: U-213, U-214, U-215
**IXC**: U-128, U-130, U-153, U-154, U-155, U-503, U-504, U-505, U-506, U-507, U-508, U-509
**XB**: U-116, U-117
**Active duty U-boats and flotillas outside the Battle of the Atlantic**
**23. Unterseebootsflottille (Salamis)**
**VIIB**: U-75
**VIIC**: U-79, U-97, U-331, U-371, U-559
**29th Unterseebootsflottille (La Spezia)**
**VIIC**: U-81, U-205

| Luftwaffe | | |
|---|---|---|
| Squadron | Base | Aircraft |
| KG-40 | Bordeaux | Fw 200 |

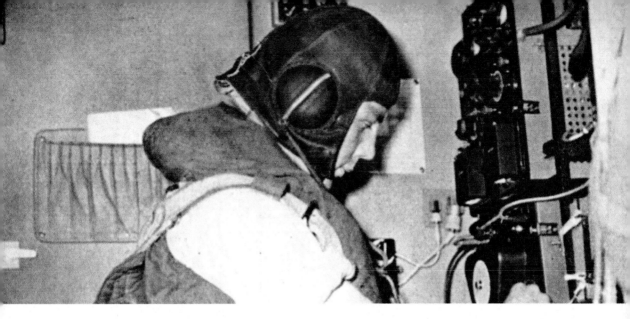

# CAMPAIGN OBJECTIVES
## The early war at sea

The campaign objectives of the Battle of the Atlantic changed dramatically between September 1939 and December 1941. It took both sides nearly a year to define their objectives. Another point of confusion was the role aircraft were to play in the Battle of the Atlantic. Use of aircraft in the Battle of the Atlantic was subsidiary to the overall campaign, but because of the nature of an air war, the air phase of the battle required different objectives to meet the overall objectives.

Part of the reason for the changing campaign was that both sides started out defining their objectives based on the experiences of the last war – World War I's Battle of the Atlantic. There was nothing wrong with this as a starting point. However, enabling technologies had changed dramatically in the 20 years between 1919 and 1939. Radios had become more reliable, torpedoes were more powerful and submarines were considerably stronger.

There were also new technologies: ASDIC and radar. ASDIC was developed during World War I, but did not see service during that conflict. It was first tested in 1920. Radar was being introduced when the war began in 1939. Neither had been tested in battle, and both sides were ignorant of the true battlefield potential of these systems. That needed to be revealed by combat.

Added to this were large portions of wishful thinking, by both sides. British and Axis leaders both attempted to fight the war they wanted to fight, rather than the war that developed. For political reasons and due to inter- (and intra-) service rivalries, both sides began by neglecting U-boats. Both sides (except perhaps for Dönitz and his U-boat arm personnel) believed U-boats would play only a subsidiary role in the naval war. They thought the battle would be decided by surface warships.

Thus both sides began the Battle of the Atlantic with the objective of using aircraft effectively against surface ships (merchant and naval) or to counter the use of enemy aircraft against surface ships. More specifically they believed (or perhaps hoped) that the Battle of the Atlantic would be settled by a series of clashes between surface warships. Over

A Hudson's radio operator sends a message. Radio communication, widely available on both aircraft and U-boats, changed the nature of submarine warfare in World War II. It permitted coordination that was impossible during World War I. (AC)

time, it became obvious that the overlooked U-boat was actually the real threat to British supply lines and trade, followed closely by long-range aircraft used against shipping.

That resulted in both sides revising their campaign objectives in late 1940. The destruction of U-boats became the primary goal of British maritime aviation, while the Germans refocused their objectives on the destruction of Allied shipping using U-boats and aircraft.

Since both offensive weapons used by the Germans were vulnerable to enemy aircraft, the air component of the campaign had asymmetrical objectives. While U-boats and Fw 200s were the objective of Allied aircraft, enemy shipping was the objective of the Germans, and evading enemy aircraft their primary objective. Success would go to the side that more clearly defined and implemented its strategic goals, but implementation – by both sides – was incomplete up to December 1941.

## Allied objectives and plans

The air component of the Battle of the Atlantic was part of a combined-arms battle involving land, sea and air forces. For Britain, the overall Battle of the Atlantic was defensive: the ultimate British goal was protection of its trade and maintaining its maritime supply lines. But the air component of the campaign was almost purely offensive. By their nature, aircraft could not hold ground, only attack or reconnoitre. Sometimes, as in fighter defence against bombers, attacking was a means of defence.

When World War II started, two organizations were responsible for protecting Britain's trade: the Royal Navy and the RAF's Coastal Command. The Royal Navy included both warships (including submarines) and aircraft. Coastal Command was a pure air force.

Coastal Command was one of three operational formations of the RAF, its maritime aviation branch. Along with Bomber Command (responsible for the RAF's strategic and tactical bombers) and Fighter Command (controlling the RAF's fighter aircraft), Coastal Command was created in 1936. In the same year, naval aircraft carried aboard ships were transferred from the RAF to the Royal Navy, creating what became the Fleet Air Arm.

In the wide waters of the Atlantic, the main mission of maritime patrol aircraft was to seek, identify and destroy enemy targets, whether surface vessels, U-boats or other maritime patrol aircraft. They were the attackers. In the context of the Battle of the Atlantic's air war, Coastal Command and FAA aircraft were attacking German U-boats

When World War II began, Coastal Command's primary focus was finding and intercepting surface warships and blockade runners. This ship, the German freighter *Morea*, was caught trying to return to Germany from Spain with its cargo of manganese. (AC)

An Avro Anson escorts a convoy in the opening month of the war. Its major purpose was to provide the convoy with early warning of and protection from raiding surface warships rather than submarines. (AC)

and patrol aircraft, which were attempting to evade the British aircraft to complete the offensive part of their missions.

Prior to World War II, the British Air Ministry, in consultation with the Royal Navy's Board of Admiralty, set trade protection, reconnaissance and cooperation with the Royal Navy as objectives for Coastal Command. As World War II began, this was interpreted as protecting ships from attacks by surface raiders (both conventional warships and disguised raiders). This was to be accomplished by maritime patrol of the North Sea's exits, both through the English Channel and through the Orkney-Shetland-Norway gap at the sea's northern exit. Fighter Command assumed responsibility for protecting British shipping from enemy aircraft in the North Sea and British coastal waters.

Anti-submarine cooperation was given secondary priority, followed by cooperation with the Navy's Northern Patrol, covering the gap between Greenland and Scotland (later known during the Cold War as the GIUK – Greenland-Iceland-UK – Gap). The nature of cooperation for these secondary and tertiary priorities went undefined. Coastal Command's attention was firmly directed towards detecting and interdicting surface traffic – enemy warships and cargo vessels – heading to Germany, rather than U-boats.

The low priority accorded to U-boats pervaded the RAF. Bomber Command bombers striking naval targets in German ports began the war forbidden to attack U-boats. This was viewed as wasting bombloads on secondary targets. The order was not cancelled until after the first week of the war, and a missed opportunity to attack several U-boats.

The FAA similarly gave U-boats a low priority. Its priorities were extending the vision of surface ships through reconnaissance, attacking enemy warships attempting to escape battle, protecting the fleet against submarines and spotting gunfire in surface actions. FAA aircraft's anti-submarine activity was defined as protecting the fleet – its battle formations – rather than protecting trade by defending convoys.

Using naval aircraft to protect merchant shipping, including the use of escort carriers – small, moderate-speed aircraft carriers converted from fast merchant vessels – was studied in the late 1930s, but little progress was achieved. In short, the FAA's primary role was protecting and aiding the Royal Navy, not Britain's trade routes.

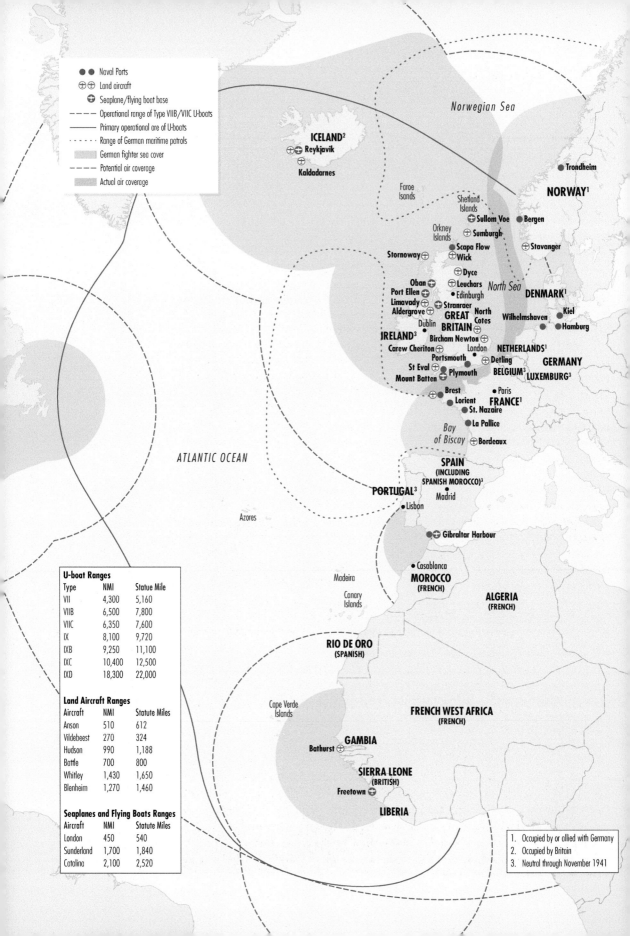

**Naval Ports** ●●

**Land aircraft** ⊕ ⊕

**Seaplane/flying boat base** ⊕

- - - Operational range of Type VIIB/VIIC U-boats

—— Primary operational are of U-boats

······ Range of German maritime patrols

German fighter sea cover

- - - Potential air coverage

Actual air coverage

*Norwegian Sea*

ICELAND[2]
⊕ Reykjavik
⊕ Kaldadarnes

● Trondheim

NORWAY[1]

Faroe Isands

Shetland Islands

⊕ Sullom Voe
● Bergen

Orkney Islands

⊕ Sumburgh
⊕ Stavanger

● Stornoway

⊕ Scapa Flow
⊕ Wick

*North Sea*

⊕ Dyce

Oban ⊕
⊕ Leuchars
DENMARK[1]

Port Ellen ⊕
● Edinburgh
● Kiel

Limavady ⊕
⊕ Stranraer
Wilhelmshaven ●
● Hamburg

Aldergrove ⊕
GREAT
North Cotes

Dublin ●
BRITAIN

IRELAND[3]
Bircham Newton
NETHERLANDS[1]

Carew Cheriton ⊕
London ●
GERMANY

St Eval ⊕
⊕ Detling
BELGIUM[3]

Mount Batten ⊕
Portsmouth ⊕
LUXEMBURG[3]

⊕ Plymouth

Brest ⊕
● Paris

● Lorient
FRANCE[1]

■ St. Nazaire

● La Pallice

*Bay of Biscay*
⊕ Bordeaux

*ATLANTIC OCEAN*

SPAIN
(INCLUDING
SPANISH MOROCCO)[3]

PORTUGAL[3]
● Madrid

*Azores*
● Lisbon

●⊕ Gibraltar Harbour

● Casablanca

MOROCCO
(FRENCH)

*Madeira*

ALGERIA
(FRENCH)

*Canary Islands*

RIO DE ORO
(SPANISH)

**U-boat Ranges**

| Type | NMI | Statue Mile |
|------|-----|-------------|
| VII | 4,300 | 5,160 |
| VIIB | 6,500 | 7,800 |
| VIIC | 6,350 | 7,600 |
| IX | 8,100 | 9,720 |
| IXB | 9,250 | 11,100 |
| IXC | 10,400 | 12,500 |
| IXD | 18,300 | 22,000 |

**Land Aircraft Ranges**

| Aircraft | NMI | Statute Miles |
|----------|-----|---------------|
| Anson | 510 | 612 |
| Vildebeest | 270 | 324 |
| Hudson | 990 | 1,188 |
| Battle | 700 | 800 |
| Whitley | 1,430 | 1,650 |
| Blenheim | 1,270 | 1,460 |

**Seaplanes and Flying Boats Ranges**

| Aircraft | NMI | Statute Miles |
|----------|-----|---------------|
| London | 450 | 540 |
| Sunderland | 1,700 | 1,840 |
| Catalina | 2,100 | 2,520 |

FRENCH WEST AFRICA
(FRENCH)

*Cape Verde Islands*

GAMBIA
Bathurst ⊕

SIERRA LEONE
(BRITISH)

Freetown ⊕

LIBERIA

1. Occupied by or allied with Germany
2. Occupied by Britain
3. Neutral through November 1941

**OPPOSITE** STRATEGIC OVERVIEW: NOVEMBER 1941

There was a measure of tailoring objectives to meet available resources in this pre-war planning. Neither the RAF nor the FAA had sufficient aircraft to meet their responsibilities, and many of the aircraft they did have were obsolescent.

Coastal Command had only one of the three groups allocated to it formed in September 1938. While it would add 13 new squadrons by the summer of 1939, it had only one modern flying boat type (the Sunderland), which had been in service less than a year. Its main maritime patrol aircraft (the Anson) lacked the range and bombload to close off the northern approaches to the North Sea. Its only strike aircraft was the obsolete Vildebeest biplane.

The FAA was in similar straits. Its main torpedo bomber/general reconnaissance aircraft was the open-cockpit Swordfish biplane. Its fighter and dive-bombing aircraft (the Fulmar, Skua and Roc) were metal monoplanes with enclosed cockpits and retracting undercarriage, but their performance could not match the first-line fighter aircraft of virtually every other nation. Often, they barely matched the performance of second-line aircraft.

To make matters worse, planned replacement aircraft were either also obsolescent or failures. The Swordfish was to be replaced by the Albacore, also a biplane, but with an enclosed cockpit. The Saro Lerwick was intended to replace Coastal Command's biplane flying boats and the Blackburn Botha was planned as a replacement for the Vildebeest torpedo bomber, but both twin-engine aircraft proved failures. Both lacked lateral stability, had poor visibility, were treacherous to fly and mechanically unreliable.

Neither organization was likely to find suitable replacements or even increase its numbers within the British aircraft industry. There was little slack production in Britain in 1938–39, and any domestic expansion was assigned to what were viewed as higher-priority production: bombers and fighters. There would not even be enough of those.

These inadequacies were due in part to the 'Ten Year Rule' that Parliament adopted in 1919 and which was not abolished until 1932. It forced Britain's armed services to base estimates on the assumption that war would not be possible for at least ten years. Even after its abolition, services could not ramp up immediately due to the global depression. Rearmament did not start until 1934, and many new factories were coming on line only in 1939. Even the unrealistically small pre-war campaign objectives were barely attainable in 1939.

The Blackburn Botha was a strike aircraft intended to replace Coastal Command's obsolete Vildebeest torpedo bombers. The Botha was so badly flawed it was quickly withdrawn from active service, leaving a gap that was hard for Coastal Command to fill. (AC)

A series of photos showing a Coastal Command attack on a U-boat. Upper left: the surfaced U-boat is spotted. Lower left: it has submerged while the aircraft lines up an attack. Right: anti-submarine bombs exploding above the U-boat. The crew claimed the U-boat was sunk, but it likely escaped undamaged. (AC)

A merchantman under construction in a British shipyard. Dönitz's tonnage war depended on his U-boats sinking ships faster than Britain could build them. Dönitz believed that with 100 U-boats at sea he could defeat Britain in 18 months. (AC)

Reality revised these campaign goals, albeit slowly. The U-boat threat became manifest on the war's first day for Britain, when the passenger liner *Athenia* was torpedoed and sunk by U-30, leading to the belief that Germany planned to resume unrestricted submarine warfare. Within a few months it became clear that the fear of surface raiders was exaggerated. The burst of activity by surface raiders when the war began was largely because they got to sea before the war started. It dwindled by the end of 1939. Additionally, the disguised raiders preferred operating in areas where aircraft were unavailable, such as the South Atlantic, Indian and Pacific oceans. Until Norway fell, it was easy to detect surface vessels transiting the North Sea with relatively few resources.

U-boats proved a different matter. It soon became obvious that they posed the real threat to British trade. The RAF then reshuffled priorities, and by January 1940 Coastal Command's highest priority was protecting shipping from U-boats. Yet although Coastal Command had made destruction of U-boats its campaign objective as early as the spring of 1940, this did not give it the resources required to achieve this objective. Moreover, FAA resources were withdrawn from the U-boat fight after HMS *Courageous* was sunk.

The war broadened in the spring of 1940, with Germany invading Norway in April and France in May. It completed its occupation of Norway in May, and forced France out of the war in June. Instead of having to seal off the North Sea, Coastal Command found itself flanked on the north by Norway and the south by German-occupied France. With Britain at risk of invasion, Coastal Command priorities were dead last.

Even once the situation stabilized, and the threat of invasion faded, RAF priorities left Coastal Command with inadequate resources. This was an intra-service issue. Most aircraft capable of long-range maritime patrol were also useful as bombers. The RAF, supported by Winston Churchill, who became Prime Minister in June when Chamberlain resigned, gave priority to the needs of Bomber Command, feeding multi-engine craft to its bombing campaign.

Thing remained fixed until March 1941, when Churchill issued his 'Battle of the Atlantic Directive'. A one-page memo, it gave the destruction of U-boats and Fw 200s the highest priority of all objectives in the Battle of the Atlantic. It called for the outfitting of ships to launch aircraft, marking a return of the FAA to the battle. It also gave priority to building up the strength of Coastal Command to protect Britain's north-western Atlantic approaches, and directed Fighter Command and Bomber Command to assist Coastal Command.

The directive provided the air forces fighting the Battle of the Atlantic with a clear goal, finally providing the priority needed to obtain necessary resources to reach that goal. Redeploying resources would take time, but by the end of 1941, Coastal Command and the FAA would be in a position to counter the U-boat and Focke-Wulf threats.

## Axis objectives and plans

No organization in Nazi Germany had clearer objectives than the Kriegsmarine's U-boat arm. Its leader, Karl Dönitz, wanted to defeat Great Britain by using his U-boats to cut Britain's supply lines and trade routes. Dönitz had a simple plan to do this: sink British merchant vessels faster than they could be replaced. Sink enough ships fast enough, and the success would reinforce success. Eventually Britain would lack resources to build enough new shipping and the deficit between the tonnage required and that available would increase in an accelerating manner with each successive month.

Dönitz's problem was that he lacked the resources to implement this vision when the war began. Additionally, especially at the beginning of World War II, he could not run the tonnage war he wished. He had to subordinate his plans to those of Admiral Erich Raeder, who commanded the Kriegsmarine in 1939. Raeder was a surface warfare proponent. Even after Dönitz demonstrated the U-boats' effectiveness, he was hobbled by micromanagement and a lack of new construction.

From the perspective of today, with the experience of World War II behind us, it is difficult to understand how anyone believed a submarine offensive against merchant shipping would be ineffective. The Germans came close to winning the Battle of the Atlantic with U-boats, United States Navy submarines shut down Imperial Japan's supply lines and British submarines successfully interdicted cargo traffic in the Mediterranean and the Skagerrak (the strait between south-east Norway and northern Denmark linking the North Sea with the Baltic).

From the perspective of the mid-1930s, however, the effectiveness of submarine warfare was unclear. While U-boats successfully blockaded Britain during parts of World War I, they were almost completely neutralized in 1918. Convoys with armed merchantmen and aerial reconnaissance eventually rendered U-boats almost completely ineffective.

Had Britain implemented convoys in 1916 there may never have been a U-boat crisis in World War I. Convoys had two effects. The first was to reduce the potential targets for U-boats to find. Instead of 50 ships sailing individually, there was one convoy of 50 ships. This reduced the opportunity for a U-boat to encounter a target by over 95 per cent. Additionally, even an unescorted convoy offered greater danger to U-boats than encountering a single armed merchant ship.

The convoy was an effective anti-submarine tool. Yet Dönitz developed tactics to overcome a convoy's strengths. Radio permitted multiple U-boats to coordinate attacks on convoys, and night-time surface attacks provided cover for attacking U-boats. (AC)

Dönitz spent the pre-war years training his U-boat crews, frequently accompanying them during training missions. Training was hard and realistic, yielding a cadre skilled in using the new tactics he developed. (AC)

Most merchant ships lost to U-boats in World War I were sunk by deck guns, not torpedoes. Generally these were unarmed ships sailing individually. Even against an individual armed merchantman, U-boat skippers preferred starting with a deck gun, because their U-boats carried few torpedoes. Against a convoy that could respond potentially with dozens of guns, using deck guns was virtually impossible. Throw in escorts armed with depth charges, and even a submerged attack using torpedoes invited destruction.

Yet aircraft, even the primitive versions of World War I, posed a greater threat to U-boats than did convoys. U-boats depended upon invisibility. They were difficult to see from the deck of a ship, and could slip in to attack range undetected. Aircraft stripped away that invisibility. Aircraft did not have to be armed: they could vector surface ships to sighted U-boats. Lighter-than-air craft were just as effective in spotting U-boats, and in 1918 convoys were often accompanied by blimps towed by one of the ships in the convoy.

The only defence U-boats had against aircraft was to submerge. Yet this rendered them ineffective. A submerged submarine was virtually immobile, slower than even an elderly tramp steamer, which, warned of the U-boat's presence by an aircraft, could escape over the horizon. Submerging also rendered a U-boat virtually blind. A U-boat's horizon as viewed through a periscope was reduced by 75 per cent from the view from the conning tower when surfaced.

Given this experience, it is unsurprising that the U-boat was viewed as obsolete as a commerce-raiding weapon by the 1930s. With the addition of ASDIC/sonar it seemed, on paper, that the trilogy of convoys, aircraft and underwater detection devices had reduced the submarine's role to an adjunct of the surface fleet, sacrificial pawns to scout and exchange for more valuable pieces on the naval chessboard. This belief was one reason every nation willingly signed the London Treaty banning unrestricted submarine warfare. Unrestricted submarine warfare was viewed as abandoning something that did not work.

Dönitz disagreed. He felt U-boats could continue to be effective commerce-raiding weapons. Submarines had improved since World War I, as well as aircraft and detection tools. U-boats were stronger than in World War I, were welded and could dive deeper. They carried more torpedoes, and these weapons were more reliable, had a longer range and a larger warhead. A single hit was likely to sink a merchant ship.

Most importantly, they had more reliable and longer-range radios than were available in 1914–18. This allowed coordination of U-boats. Unlike during World War I, where U-boats patrolled independently, Dönitz planned to direct them from land. U-boats were to make daily reports of their position and report convoy sightings. Dönitz and his staff would collate these reports, and then combine outside intelligence (Luftwaffe sightings and signal intelligence) to direct U-boats to profitable hunting areas.

This countered one advantage of convoys. Convoys were most effective against individual U-boats acting independently. Setting patrol lines of U-boats increased the odds of a convoy being sighted. Once sighted, Dönitz would have all the patrol line's U-boats converge on the convoy. Multiple U-boats would then make a coordinated attack, overwhelming the escorts. He called this *Rudeltaktik*, or pack tactics. The Allies called it wolf-pack tactics.

Dönitz also recognized ASDIC's major weakness: it only identified submerged U-boats. A surfaced U-boat was invisible to an ASDIC receiver. He thus developed a doctrine of attacking at night, while surfaced. Low in the water, the U-boat was almost impossible to spot in the dark, while surface ships, especially merchant ships, would be clearly silhouetted against the horizon. The U-boat would approach, fire a spread of torpedoes, and submerge only after its presence was detected. Combined with *Rudeltaktik*, it should leave the escorts too busy to concentrate on any single U-boat.

Dönitz had no pre-war counter for anti-submarine aircraft. Rather, he counted on two things. The ocean was big. A large number of aircraft were needed to spot a small amount of U-boats. Also, he depended on the night to shield his U-boats when attacking. When the war started, there was no reliable way to detect U-boats in the dark. Aircraft could carry flares, but not enough to provide continual lighting during a patrol. They could drop them if they detected a U-boat, but not until then.

Ultimately, although he tried several different tactics, Dönitz found no effective defence against aircraft. The only tool available to U-boats was evasion, generally by submerging once aircraft were detected. For most of the first two years of the war, this was enough.

As stated above, winning the tonnage war that Dönitz envisioned meant sinking more ships than Britain could replace. British shipyards could produce up to 1,250,000 tons of ships annually. While some of that construction was going into warships, it meant that Germany's U-boats were faced with the task of sinking 100,000 tons of merchant shipping each month – roughly 25 ships. This was achievable, but neglected ship construction in the United States.

Dönitz did not have a total of 100 U-boats operational until 1941, much less 100 at sea at one time. The bottleneck was U-boat construction. It was painfully slow, with fewer than 60 U-boats entering service by December 1940. (AC)

Even before entering World War II, US shipyards were building nearly 100,000 tons of merchant shipping each month – all of which could potentially be used to carry British cargos. It was also not enough to simply sink more ships than the British could build. The U-boats had to whittle away at the merchant marine that already existed in September 1939. There were over 6,000 ocean-going merchant ships on the world's seas, totalling over 60 million tons. Thus, while sinking 100,000 tons per month kept the British merchant fleets from growing, the U-boats would have to average 300,000 tons per month to bring Britain to its knees. That assumed construction levels – of both the belligerent Allies and neutral nations – remained no higher than 2 million tons annually.

Achieving that objective was a numbers game. Assuming a U-boat averaged sinking three ships per war patrol, sinking 75 ships per month required 25 U-boats at sea each month. Since only a third of the active U-boat force could be at sea at one time (with a third preparing to sail and another third receiving maintenance after a patrol), Dönitz's vision required a fleet of at least 75 ocean-going (Type VII and IX) U-boats. Dönitz wanted to start the war with 300, so that 100 could be at sea continuously.

Dönitz's first battle in his tonnage war was convincing the German government to drop the London Submarine Protocol and adopt unrestricted submarine warfare. He was largely unsuccessful during 1939, and it took until August 1940 before his U-boats were completely relieved from the London Protocol. His next challenge was getting enough U-boats to reach his tonnage war goals, which took most of the first two years of the war. The construction tap was finally opening by mid-1941.

Dönitz's final challenge was keeping enough U-boats in the Atlantic to fight his tonnage war. Here he was ultimately unsuccessful. Subject to the whims of Adolf Hitler, he was often forced to strip his Atlantic U-boats for other purposes. The most egregious example took place in the last quarter of 1941, when he was ordered to send 28 U-boats to the Mediterranean, a sea largely devoid of merchant shipping.

# THE CAMPAIGN

A Saro London. Introduced in 1936, the London was the most modern flying boat the RAF had until the introduction of the Sunderland in 1938. Thirty-one were built and employed in two Coastal Command squadrons.

**'For if the trumpet gives an uncertain sound, who shall prepare himself for the battle?'**

1st Corinthians, Chapter 14, Verse 8, *King James Bible*

The Battle of the Atlantic started in 1939 and raged until the end of World War II. Preparations for the battle began four years earlier, in June 1935, when Nazi Germany commissioned its first U-boat. A year later, Britain's Royal Air Force established Coastal Command, one of whose responsibilities was anti-submarine warfare.

Despite having years to prepare for a new battle for control of the seas around Britain, both sides entered the war unprepared. The Germans were unready to wage a war against British commerce, whether with surface raiders or submarines. Britain, although it believed it was ready to defeat the U-boat threat, was equally not prepared to effectively counter the U-boat.

For no part of Britain's defence forces was this more true than with what should have been its most effective anti-submarine force – Coastal Command and its maritime patrol aircraft. Initially its aircraft lacked weapons capable of sinking U-boats. If Coastal Command could have sunk U-boats at the rate they did in late 1941, Germany's U-boat fleet could well have been eliminated by early 1940.

Despite the weakness of Britain's air defences against its U-boats, Germany proved equally unable to exploit this failure. It lacked the number of U-boats required to take Britain out of the war, and did not have the shipbuilding capacity to build U-boats at much more than a replacement rate.

The result was that both nations spent the first two years of the Battle of the Atlantic preparing to win the battle. During this period Britain built the tools needed for its aircraft to destroy the U-boat threat, while Germany ramped up production of U-boats and crew training to a point where the U-boat force could be decisive. Yet although the first two years of the Battle of the Atlantic was a time of fumbling and lost opportunity, it laid foundations that determined which side would win and which side would lose.

# Origins – 1935–39

On 29 June 1935, the German Kriegsmarine commissioned its first U-boat, U-1. The ceremony was public, the new submarine coming shortly after the German Navy was renamed from Reichsmarine (State Navy) to Kriegsmarine (War Navy).

Germany was forbidden submarines by the Versailles Treaty, signed in 1919. Despite this, Germany continued secret development of submarines throughout the 1920s and early 1930s, building prototypes in Spain and Finland. Yet the 250-ton U-1 did not represent German defiance of international treaties. The boat was built in accordance with the new Anglo-German Naval Agreement signed just weeks earlier.

This treaty permitted Germany to build capital ships up to 35 per cent of the tonnage allowed to Great Britain under the 1930 London Naval Treaty. It also allowed Germany to build submarines to parity with the Royal Navy, although Germany pledged to build only 45 per cent of that tonnage. In exchange, Germany agreed to abide by the 1930 London Naval Treaty's Submarine Protocol, Article 22 of which barred unrestricted submarine warfare against merchant shipping.

Why did Britain agree to permit Germany submarines? The reason was simple: Britain felt submarines no longer posed a significant threat to merchant shipping. The World War I U-boat threat had been quickly neutered in 1918 after the adoption of convoys and widespread use of anti-submarine aircraft. The capabilities of anti-submarine aircraft had increased dramatically since 1918. They could now carry larger bombloads, over longer distances and in more reliable aircraft.

The introduction of ASDIC cemented British certainty that the submarine would be ineffective against merchant shipping. Pre-war tests indicated it was 80 per cent effective at

Three U-boats of the 1. 'Wedingen' Flotille. The first U-boat flotilla formed after Germany was permitted to have U-boats again, it was named after a World War I submarine ace. (AC)

detecting submarines. It was believed that a lone submarine making an underwater attack against a defended convoy protected by ASDIC would have a short life.

Admiral Raeder agreed with this assessment. His plans for the Kriegsmarine centred on big surface warships. Submarines, along with destroyers and other auxiliaries, would merely support the battleships. He envisioned the U-boat's function as scouting for the battle fleet. He assigned command of the reconstituted U-boat arm to Fregattenkapitän (Commander) Karl Dönitz.

Dönitz commanded a U-boat during World War I. Although initially reluctant to return to U-boats, once in charge he developed his command with enthusiasm. While acknowledging anti-submarine developments, he felt the U-boat was still a capable weapon. The 1935 U-boat was stronger and more reliable than that of 1918, could dive deeper and move faster, both surfaced and underwater. Its torpedoes were more powerful, with a warhead nearly double that of the World War I weapon. Additionally, Germany had a wakeless electric-powered torpedo. Combined with new tactics for using U-boats (the so-called wolf packs), Dönitz felt he could turn the U-boat into a war-winning weapon.

Unfortunately for Germany, Dönitz failed to persuade Raeder or Hitler of this vision, so the U-boats remained auxiliary to the large surface ships. There was only a modest build-up of the U-boat force prior to World War II. There were 15 U-boats in commission at the end of 1935, 21 more were added in 1936, only one in 1937 and ten in 1938.

Dönitz also lost the struggle to get the type of U-boats he wanted built. Where he favoured the 500-ton Type VII design, when Germany entered World War II well over half of its U-boats were the 250-ton Type II. These small boats were good for training, but were too small to operate beyond the North Sea or Baltic Sea. Additional pre-war tonnage was allocated to four Type XI 'U-cruisers', monstrous vessels displacing 3,600 tons. This tonnage could have gone to building 28 Type VII or 19 Type IX boats. (These U-cruisers were cancelled after the war began.)

Within these limitations, Dönitz built an effective submarine force. He organized the U-boats into flotillas, adding more as the number of U-boats grew. The first flotilla was named after Otto Weddigen, who sank the British armoured cruisers HMS *Aboukir*, *Cressy* and *Hogue* in September 1914. Subsequent flotillas were named after other famous World War I U-boat skippers. By 1939 there were seven, including a training flotilla.

The training was rigorous. The boats went to sea often, and practised continuously. A boat might conduct eight daytime submerged attack practices and six night surface attack drills each day, with training conducted five days a week.

Maximum depth diving drills were regularly conducted – at least until one U-boat experienced a structural problem at test depth. Thereafter, at the orders of Kriegsmarine high command, dive depths were limited to 45 metres. Dönitz protested, believing training had to emulate wartime, but could not get the limitation lifted.

Despite this, by 1939 Dönitz built a small but credible U-boat force. It was manned by competent crews, skilled and motivated officers and a dedicated staff. Due to Dönitz's leadership, there was close camaraderie between officers and men. They were well trained, with regular exercises held in the Baltic practicing *Rudeltaktik* wolf-pack attacks on

U-25 (pictured) was one of two Type I U-boats commissioned by the Kriegsmarine. Based on a Spanish design, it was the first attempt by the Kriegsmarine to build an ocean-going submarine. (AC)

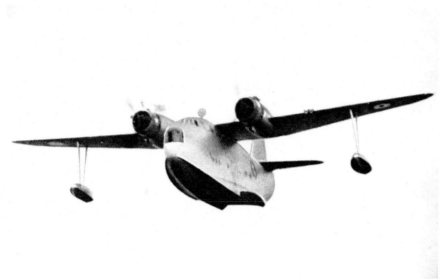

Realizing the obsolescence of their existing twin-engine flying boats, Coastal Command had Sanders-Roe (Saro) rush a replacement into production. First flown in November 1938, the aircraft, named the Lerwick, looked impressive but proved a failure. (AC)

simulated convoys. The infrastructure was in place to allow Dönitz to direct his U-boats in coordinated attacks against British merchantmen. (Dönitz believed Article 22 would quickly become a dead letter.)

It was anticipated that by 1942 his U-boat force would total 118 U-boats, which would increase to 249 by 1945, when Germany expected to go to war with Great Britain. This number of U-boats was less than the 300 Dönitz required to win his tonnage war, but it was close. However, only 160 would be the Type VIIs and Type IXs needed for the war that he planned. The rest were to be coastal Type IIs or very large minelaying or cruiser U-boats, unsuitable for mid-Atlantic attacks against heavily defended convoys. In January 1939 Dönitz, newly promoted to Kommodore, believed he had six years to shape the force better to his liking before the war started.

British preparation for a future Battle of the Atlantic began on 14 July 1936 with a reorganization of the RAF. The RAF was transformed into three operational 'commands': Bomber, Fighter and Coastal Command. Bomber Command coordinated all bombing activities and Fighter Command controlled all fighter activities within the RAF. Coastal

A design submitted by Lockheed resulted in Coastal Command signing a contract for the Hudson in June 1938. First deliveries began in February 1939. This shows the Hudson assembly line in Burbank, California. (AC)

Command's mission was less straightforward. It was responsible for all maritime air power activities within the RAF. This included maritime reconnaissance, convoy protection and anti-shipping action. It required aircraft capable of conducting reconnaissance, providing anti-submarine and anti-surface vessel capability, and providing defence against enemy aircraft.

Coastal Command faced several challenges in meeting its objectives. Anti-submarine aircraft had been almost totally neglected, an action prompted by budget constraints and justified by ASDIC reducing the submarine threat. This also led to neglect of air-dropped anti-submarine bombs and depth charges. A parsimonious Air Ministry believed the Royal Navy would deal with submarines.

The inherited resources of its immediate predecessor, Coastal Area, were several squadrons of largely obsolete aircraft. Replacement aircraft were slowly allocated to Coastal Command, starting with the Avro Anson. Number 48 Squadron began equipping with the Anson in March 1936, when it was still part of Coastal Area. Three more squadrons were equipped with the Anson in 1937. Intended as a light bomber, the Anson eventually equipped ten Coastal Command squadrons by September 1939.

Other new aircraft joined Coastal Command. The Air Ministry ordered the Short Sunderland as a long-range patrol aircraft in 1936, and it entered service in 1938. By 1939 three Sunderland squadrons were active. Development of the Bristol Beaufort and Blackburn Botha torpedo bombers also began in 1936, as did that of the twin-engine Saro Lerwick flying boat. All three were to enter service in 1939. Meanwhile, Coastal Command soldiered on with open-cockpit biplanes for maritime strike and medium-range water-based reconnaissance.

While the size of the rest of the RAF doubled between July 1936 and March 1939, Coastal Command grew little. Budgets constrained expansion and Coastal Command was viewed as less important than Bomber or Fighter Commands. Coastal Command even shrank, losing the carrier-based squadrons, which were being transferred to the Royal Navy as the result of an agreement reached between the Admiralty and the Air Ministry in 1936.

The handover began in 1937 and was completed in May 1939. Aircrew in those squadrons could remain with the RAF or transfer to the Royal Navy. The Air Ministry saw the transfer as no loss, while the Royal Navy viewed it as a major gain. The RAF was unenthusiastic about carrier aircraft. Between 1929 and 1932 it procured only 18 carrier aircraft. The Royal Navy, meanwhile, was expanding its carrier fleet. In addition to the six carriers it acquired between 1916 and 1930, it added a new aircraft carrier in 1937 and laid down six new fleet carriers between 1936 and 1939. The Fleet Air Arm badly needed expansion to provide air groups for those ships, and it required more modern aircraft than it was able to procure when the Air Ministry was in charge of procurement.

Coastal Command did grow organizationally. When formed in 1936, it consisted of just 15 Group; 16 Group and 17 Group (a training group) formed in December 1936, and 18 Group followed in August 1938. This gave Coastal Command three operational groups (15, 16 and 18) and one training group (17). When war broke out, 15 Group had responsibility for the Western Approaches, 16 Group for the English Channel and southern North Sea, while 18 Group covered Britain's northern waters. In August 1937 Air Marshall Sir Frederick Bowhill took command of Coastal Command, a position he would hold until mid-1941.

While Coastal Command grew slowly in 1936 and 1937, growth accelerated in 1938. German aggression convinced Parliament that rearmament was necessary, yet it was apparent that Britain's need for aircraft exceeded the capabilities of its aircraft industry. Short could only deliver two Sunderlands per month. The Admiralty predicted a need for 50 torpedo bombers (Swordfish and Albacores) per month to maintain their numbers once war broke out, but it forecast production rates at just 20–26 per month.

Lerwick, Botha and Beaufort production was expected to start in late 1939. Increased Anson production was undesirable. A cutting-edge design in 1933, the Anson was by now outdated. So much of the domestic aircraft industry was devoted to heavy bomber and fighter production that Coastal Command's needs could not be met. Short was building the Stirling heavy bomber as well as the Sunderland, and the Stirling was viewed as more important. Similarly, Supermarine, which built flying boats in the 1930s, was also building the critical Spitfire fighter.

Recognizing the need for more aircraft, the Air Ministry sent a mission to North America in 1938 to obtain aircraft built in the United States and Canada. The aircraft industry in the United States proved eager suppliers to the RAF (and later France and Norway). Lockheed, in Burbank, California, was especially hungry for orders. The Commission visited Lockheed seeking a navigation trainer version of the Lockheed Model 14 airliner.

Learning of Britain's need for maritime reconnaissance aircraft, Lockheed prepared a bomber version mock-up prior to the visit. When the Commission criticized the design, Lockheed modified the mock-up overnight, incorporating the desired changes. Impressed, the Commission ordered the bomber, dubbed the Hudson. The contract was signed in June 1938, and the first deliveries arrived in Britain in February 1939. The first Hudson squadron became operational in June that year, just in time to patrol the North Sea exit in to the Atlantic between Scotland and Norway.

By September 1939 Coastal Command had grown to 19 squadrons: 11 land-based general reconnaissance squadrons (ten flying Ansons, one Hudsons), seven flying boat squadrons (three with Sunderlands, four with various biplanes) and two strike squadrons (equipped with the obsolete biplane Vildebeest torpedo bombers). The strike squadrons had no anti-submarine capacity, leaving 17 squadrons to meet the U-boat menace.

## The first round: September 1939 to June 1940

The opening of World War II caught both sides unprepared for a new Battle of the Atlantic. Hitler did not believe Britain and France would go to war over Poland, thinking they would back down at the last minute. They had on every previous German land grab, from the remilitarization of the Rhineland in March 1936 through to the occupation of Czechoslovakia in March 1939. Hitler's military build-up was incomplete, with the Kriegsmarine only starting the expansion envisioned under the 'Z' plan, which envisioned the re-equipping and growth of German naval forces to match the Royal Navy by 1948.

Britain was similarly unprepared. It, too, was only beginning its rearmament. Coastal Command and the FAA were lagging behind other organizations in the build-up. Coastal Command's Hudson squadrons were only just becoming available for use. While the Lerwick and Botha were finally coming off the assembly lines, there were no active squadrons flying these. The Anson and every flying boat, except the Sunderland, were unsatisfactory.

As for the FAA, not only were there too few aircraft and aircrew, but available aircraft were inadequate. The torpedo bombers were outdated, and the FAA's dive bomber (the Skua) and its fighters (Fulmar and Roc) were inferior to similar carrier aircraft of other navies. Although neither Coastal Command nor the FAA yet realized it, they had no effective weapons against U-boats. The 100lb anti-shipping bombs could not crack a U-boat's hull, the 250lb bomb required a direct hit and only the Sunderland could carry the air-droppable 450lb depth charge.

In August 1939 Dönitz had only 57 U-boats in commission, with four fitting out and 16 under construction. Another 41 were on order. Only 28 commissioned U-boats were ocean-going designs displacing 500 tons or more. Twenty-nine were various Type II 250-ton boats. He sent his boats to sea from 19 August, before the scheduled invasion of Poland, against a potential British declaration of war. He had conducted similar mobilizations prior to previous crises, viewing them as valuable practice if war broke out. This time it did.

Reserving four Type II and three Type VII U-boats for action in the Baltic, Dönitz sent the rest to battle stations in the North Sea and North Atlantic. Three Type II boats were sent to patrol the Kattegat, connecting the Baltic and North Seas between Denmark and Sweden. Thirteen Type IIs were sent into the North Sea, while 19 Type IA, VII and IX U-boats were assigned sectors in the North Atlantic Ocean, covering the south-west and north-west Approaches to the British Isles. A few others were held in port as reserves.

Coastal Command aircraft began patrolling the North Sea and English Channel on 24 August as the two nations began to slide towards war. Their main mission was not hunting U-boats, but rather detecting Kriegsmarine warships exiting the North Sea and tracking German merchant shipping traversing these waters. They had missed the warships, which passed through the aerial cordon before 24 August.

When Germany invaded Poland on 1 September 1939, Britain issued an ultimatum demanding German withdrawal from Poland. It was ignored. Britain then declared war on Germany on 3 September. At 1530hrs, Dönitz issued orders for U-boats to attack British shipping.

The Kriegsmarine began World War II observing London Treaty prize rules. This U-boat was photographed examining the neutral US freighter *Wacosta* on 9 September 1939. *Wacosta* was allowed to proceed to New York after three hours. (AC)

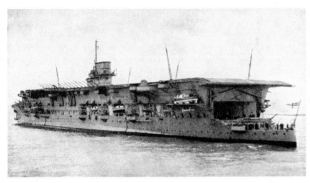

The U-boats were hobbled, however. Hitler was hoping Britain and France could be talked into making peace after his troops conquered Poland, so he ordered U-boats to observe the 1930 Submarine Protocol. Except for troopships, warships and ships in convoy, ships were not to be sunk without warning. Instead, U-boats had to surface and stop merchant ships, sinking them only after the crew abandoned the vessel. Additionally, no French-flagged ships were to be sunk, which Hitler hoped could convince France to make peace separately.

At 1940hrs, a U-boat, U-30, patrolling west of Scotland saw what it assumed was a Royal Navy auxiliary cruiser and attacked it without warning. Two torpedoes were fired. One struck and sank the ship. It was the passenger liner *Athenia*, heading to Canada with civilians fleeing the war. The liner was notionally protected from attack without warning by Hitler's orders. Britain was thus convinced that Germany planned unlimited submarine warfare and behaved accordingly. The Battle of the Atlantic had begun.

At first it seemed British predictions about the U-boats being manageable were correct. U-boats sank 48 belligerent and neutral merchant ships in September 1939, but many were ships sailing independently when the war began. October saw 33 ships sunk by U-boats, with 27 in November and 39 in December. Merchant losses totalled 509,321 tons in 1939. This was high, but acceptable, especially as the trend seemed to be going the right way.

In exchange, nine U-boats were lost, with two in September, five in October and one each in November and December. None were sunk by aircraft. Three struck British mines, one was torpedoed by a Royal Navy submarine and five were sunk by surface escort ships. Aircraft – FAA and Coastal Command – sank none, and did not even participate in any U-boat sinkings.

Coastal Command was active however. In September it spent nearly 2,000 hours flying convoy support and 5,500 hours conducting general reconnaissance. Through to the end of 1939 it spent 8,278 hours supporting convoys and 13,080 hours on aerial patrols. Coastal Command aircraft spotted 51 U-boats in 1939, 27 of them in September, and attacked 46 of the U-boats spotted. However, especially in September and October, the focus of Coastal Command's efforts was spent seeking German warships and homeward-bound German freighters, not U-boats. Not until mid-November were detecting and attacking U-boats given equal priority with seeking surface raiders.

Even without sinking U-boats, Coastal Command was forcing U-boats to submerge, something which reduced their effectiveness. They also assisted in the recovery of shipwreck survivors. In September two Sunderlands rescued the crew of the *Kensington Court*, sunk in the South-western Approaches. Landing mid-ocean, they recovered 35 survivors and flew them to safety. It made headlines, but raised unrealistic expectations about the ability to recover sinking victims.

An even worse performance was turned in by the FAA. Due to the lack of long-range Coastal Command patrol aircraft, there were gaps in air coverage in the south-western

HMS *Courageous* was part of a hunter-killer group hunting U-boats in the South-west Approaches in September 1939. On 17 September the hunter was torpedoed and sunk by U-29, one of the U-boats it was hunting. (AC)

When the *Kensington Court* was torpedoed and sunk by U-32, its 35 survivors were picked up by two Sunderland flying boats and flown to safety in Britain. (AC)

When the *Kensington Court* was torpedoed and sunk by U-32, its 35 survivors were picked up by two Sunderland flying boats and flown to safety in Britain. (AC)

and north-western Approaches, the Atlantic approaches to the English Channel and North Channel respectively. The Royal Navy attempted covering these gaps with carrier aircraft, stationing HMS *Ark Royal* in the north-western Approaches and HMS *Courageous* in the south-western Approaches.

The experiment proved disastrous. On 14 September, while on anti-submarine patrol, *Ark Royal*'s aircraft spotted a surfaced U-30 sinking the freighter *Fanad Head*. Three Skuas and three Swordfish attacked U-30, but succeeded only in destroying two Skuas with their own bombs. Three destroyers from *Ark Royal*'s escorts arrived and attacked the by-then submerged U-30. While damaging the U-boat, they did not sink it. Later that day, *Ark Royal* was attacked by U-39. It was saved only because the torpedo's magnetic trigger exploded prematurely. *Ark Royal*'s escorts sank U-39. Although the British believed they bagged two U-boats in one day, using Britain's newest aircraft carrier as bait appeared ill advised.

How ill-advised this was would be demonstrated three days later. *Courageous* was patrolling the approaches to the English Channel, its aircraft protecting a homeward-bound convoy. Its Swordfish spotted and attacked U-59, forcing the U-boat under but failing to sink it, despite hitting it with 100lb anti-submarine bombs. The Swordfish were spotted by a submerged U-29 as they returned to the carrier.

Alerted, U-29 began searching. Chance brought *Courageous* within range of U-29, whose skipper, Otto Schuhart, fired his last two torpedoes at the carrier, then dived deep. Both torpedoes struck, sinking *Courageous*, which went down with 519 men of a crew of 1,260. Schuhart survived a heavy depth-charging to return to Wilhelmshaven a hero. Thereafter the Royal Navy withdrew its fleet carriers from anti-submarine patrols. The FAA thus retired from U-boat hunting for the next two years.

Even without the FAA, it appeared Britain's surface warships and Coastal Command were containing the U-boats. Ship losses went up during the winter months, with their long nights – Dönitz's emphasis on night-time surface attack paying dividends – yet the number of sinkings went back down as spring approached.

Coastal Command's main challenge seemed to be getting enough aircraft to fulfill its duties. It began using De Havilland Moth biplanes on Britain's eastern coast, in the hope that U-boats would submerge when the aircraft were spotted. Bomber Command lent Coastal Command squadrons for maritime reconnaissance, generally reluctantly and almost always squadrons flying the oldest bombers operational – aircraft that would not be missed over Germany.

The mystery of why U-boats were unharmed by frequent aircraft attacks was finally solved in December 1939. HMS *Snapper*, a British submarine, was mistaken for a U-boat and bombed by a Coastal Command aircraft. *Snapper* took a direct hit on the conning tower with a 100lb bomb. It survived to make port and lodge an angry protest.

This meant the only aircraft capable of sinking a U-boat were Hudsons and Sunderlands. The Hudson could drop sticks of 250lb bombs, which could crack a U-boat's hull but only with a direct hit, and the Sunderland both the 250lb anti-submarine bomb and the 450lb depth charge. An air-droppable 250lb depth charge was ordered in January 1940, but it would take over a year before it saw service.

Hudson numbers were increasing. Lockheed delivered the last of the first 200, originally contracted in October, two months early. The order was expanded to 351, and eventually the Commonwealth received over 3,100 Hudsons. The first Botha and Lerwick squadrons were formed in late 1939. The aircraft were equally quickly withdrawn, although the Lerwick would be brought back briefly before being retired in mid-1940.

That a Coastal Command desperately short of aircraft would remove them was testimony to their shortcomings. The Lerwick could not hold altitude or fly in a straight line with one engine out. Losing an engine doomed the aircraft to fly in ever-descending circles, a trait highly undesirable in a long-range ocean patrol aircraft. They were to be replaced by the US-built Consolidated Catalina, but deliveries of those did not start until the spring of 1941.

Dönitz would have appreciated Coastal Command's inventory problems, as he lacked the U-boats to carry out the tonnage war he desired. By January 1940 he had only 32 active U-boats, fewer than he started the war with. New construction was not keeping up with the losses. U-boats at sea were sinking ships at a satisfying rate, but there simply were not enough U-boats available.

Two bits of good news for Coastal Command arrived in January 1940. The first airborne air search radar (ASV, or air search, vessel) became operational in January. ASV Mk I radars were installed in Hudsons, although they were so crude they were mainly used to locate convoys. Also, a 228 Squadron Sunderland, in cooperation with HMS *Whitshed* and

# Skuas Down

At the outset of World War II, the Royal Navy attempted to use a hunter killer group centred on an aircraft carrier. One result was a tragicomic attack which saw two Blackburn Skuas off HMS *Ark Royal* destroyed by their own anti-submarine bombs while attacking U-30.

The unescorted freighter *Fanad Head* was spotted by U-30. The Germans surfaced, then, following prize rules, ordered the freighter's crew to abandon the ship. To conserve torpedoes, U-30's skipper sent two men aboard *Fanad Head* to scuttle it with demolition charges. They reached the ship on an inflatable rubber dinghy, which was tied to the U-boat by a long rope.

*Fanad Head* had radioed a report of the submarine attack and its location, and it was within range of aircraft of an anti-submarine task force built around *Ark Royal*. Three Skua fighter/dive bombers were sent in search of the U-boat.

The first Skua reached the site, saw the U-boat and dropped a 100lb anti-submarine bomb on it. The bomb bounced into mid-air and exploded. Fragments hit the aircraft, forcing it to ditch. Both Skua crewmen escaped, badly burned. One drowned, but the pilot was saved by a German who dived into the water to rescue him. Meanwhile, U-30 submerged, trailing the dinghy on the surface.

It resurfaced just as the second Skua reached the scene and dropped its bomb on what it thought was the sub's conning tower, but was more likely the rubber raft or wreckage of the first Skua. That bomb was a dud. The Skua then strafed the surfaced U-30, which dived again as the second Skua flew away.

U-30 resurfaced to recover its crewmen, just as the third Skua arrived and also attacked the U-boat. The bomb again skipped into the air, this time exploding close enough for the blast to rip off the nose of the Skua.

This plate shows the climax of these misadventures, with the third Skua blowing its own nose off. Its pilot was rescued by the Germans, and both RAF pilots spent the war as POWs.

Type IX U-boat U-37 returns to port on 8 November 1939 after a successful patrol. It sank eight ships totalling 35,305 tons. It flies a pennant with the name of each kill from its mast. (AC)

HMS *Fowey*, caused the sinking of U-55. The Sunderland bombed U-55, which was unable to submerge after damage received from the ships, leading the crew to scuttle the U-boat. It was Coastal Command's first kill.

Although German U-boats sank 53 vessels in January 1940 and 50 in February, the numbers plummeted in March and April, with just 26 and 6 merchant ships sunk respectively, while May saw only 15 ships lost. It was beginning to look like Britain had mastered the U-boat threat, but it was a false dawn. The reason Atlantic losses plummeted was that Dönitz withdrew the U-boats to support a late-April invasion of Denmark and Norway. That invasion succeeded in sidelining most of the Kriegsmarine's surface fleet, but it only cost two U-boats, one of which was sunk by a Swordfish. It also succeeded in capturing Norway, neatly flanking the British guarding the northern approaches to the North Sea.

Worse followed, as Germany invaded France on 10 May 1940. By 4 June Britain had withdrawn its troops from northern France. On 22 June France signed an armistice with Germany, ceding German occupation of French provinces bordering the English Channel and Atlantic coast. Whereas Britain had largely succeeded in penning U-boats in the North Sea by March 1940, the U-boats now had bases in Norway and France. The scope of the Battle of the Atlantic had widened dramatically.

## The wider war: June 1940 to October 1940

The fall of France so soon after the German capture of Norway changed the Battle of the Atlantic. It opened the Atlantic to U-boats, providing Germany with ports on the French Atlantic coast and in Norway. This dramatically increased the U-boats' operational radius, eliminating the 1,000-nautical-mile round trip from Germany's North Sea ports to the Atlantic. French Atlantic or Norwegian harbours increased the time spent in the Atlantic by one-eighth, allowing U-boats to operate 500 nautical miles further west than they had when confined to German ports.

It also allowed free passage from Germany to the French Atlantic coast. When the Allies held both coasts of the English Channel, U-boats had to run a gauntlet of hostile minefields and patrolling aircraft. With Germany holding the French coast, they could move behind German-laid minefields, protected from British aircraft by Luftwaffe fighters.

German occupation of France and Norway also constrained Britain. Luftwaffe air power closed the English Channel and North Sea to British commerce. Britain continued coastal convoys over the summer for prestige purposes before reality led to their termination. The new geography forced the abandonment of London and Southampton as ports for Atlantic cargoes. Instead, shipping was routed to Liverpool and Glasgow.

Britain also faced more enemies. Italy entered the war as a German ally on 10 June, which forced Britain to send military and naval resources to the Mediterranean and Red Sea. Italian submarines also joined German U-boats in the North Atlantic. After Britain neutralized French naval assets outside metropolitan France, by seizing French warships in Britain and Egypt, forcing demilitarization of French warships in the West Indies, and attacking the French fleets at Mers-el-Kebir and Dakar in July and September 1940 France became a hostile neutral.

Although the Battle of the Atlantic remained important, it was necessarily a lower priority than Britain's survival. To block Germany after it invaded Denmark – which controlled both the Faroe Islands and Iceland – Britain occupied the Faroes in April and Iceland in May. However, Britain had no other resources besides small Royal Marine contingents to do so, as everything was needed in Britain to forestall a German invasion expected that summer or early autumn. Coastal Command strike aircraft, which might have been used for maritime

A U-boat caught on the surface by a Coastal Command aircraft is photographed as it makes a hasty dive. (AC)

patrols, were reserved for invasion response. Not until having won the Battle of Britain by the end of September, with the threat of German invasion having receded, could more resources be allocated to Coastal Command.

For Dönitz the summer period represented an opportunity. Hitler had been gradually lifting restrictions on U-boats throughout the first six months of 1940. By June, any merchantman except friendly neutrals (by June 1940, Spain, Japan and Russia) within 100 nautical miles of Britain could be attacked without warning. In August all restrictions were lifted.

In June, with his U-boats released from Norwegian operations, Dönitz decided to experiment with wolf packs. In mid-June he set up two – the seven-boat Wolf Pack Prien covering the Western Approaches west of Scotland, and the five-boat Wolf Pack Rosing west of Cape Finisterre.

Wolf Pack Prien was led by Günther Prien, a U-boat ace who penetrated Scapa Flow in 1939 and sank the battleship HMS *Royal Oak*. It intercepted Convoy HX-47, sinking three ships from the convoy and two others steaming independently. Wolf Pack Rosing, named after its senior U-boat captain, Hans Rosing, intercepted the Sierra Leone Convoy SL-34 heading to Britain from West Africa. Two ships from the convoy were sunk, as well as two others sailing independently.

These would be the last wolf packs for nearly a year. The *Rudeltaktik* worked, but they were unnecessary. For the next 12 months, U-boats operating independently could sink more ships than they could in a pack. Destroyer losses suffered during the Norway campaign and the Dunkirk evacuation, as well as construction delays, left Britain short of escort vessels. Many surviving destroyers were being held in England to counter any German invasion attempt. This led to few available escorts.

Frequently convoys had only three or four escorts, sometimes just one or two. This permitted individual U-boats to attack convoys and slip away unmolested. There were too few escorts to maintain contact with a detected U-boat and still protect the convoy.

Another factor was that wolf packs were more effective against convoys than independently operating vessels. In 1939 and 1940, convoys were only maintained to 12.5 degrees west

The Kriegsmarine started using Lorient in Brittany as a U-boat base in July 1940. It began construction of the submarine pens shown in this drawing in September 1940 and became the location of Dönitz's headquarters in November. (USNHHC)

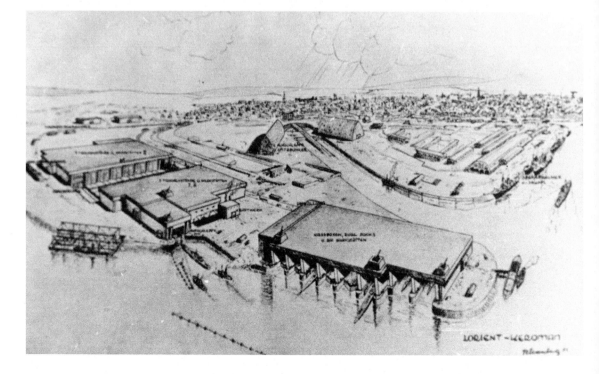

Italy joined the German Axis in June 1940, operating submarines from French bases that autumn. Six, including the Calvi-class submarine *Giuseppe Finzi* (pictured, photographed from an US freighter), arrived at Bordeaux in September. (USNHHC)

longitude. West of that, outbound convoys broke up and ships sailed independently. The escorts would pick up eastward-bound ships at that longitude and escort them to British west coast ports. That longitude was chosen because it was the effective western operational boundary for U-boats departing German ports. Restricting escorts to areas where U-boats operated permitted better use of the limited escorts the Royal Navy had. If no U-boats were present, there was no need to protect merchantmen from them.

By July 1940 this location had been moved to 17 degrees west, 300 nautical miles west of Ireland. However, it was not far enough west. With French ports now available to U-boats, they could easily cruise the waters south of Iceland. The escort limit was shifted another two degrees west, but that was as far as British escorts could sail due to fuel limitations until Iceland had port facilities.

Nor could Coastal Command help. Hudsons had an operational radius of 450nm, so could not effectively escort convoys further than surface escorts. While Sunderlands had an operational radius of 850nm, there were too few to provide continuous escort. Coastal Command forced U-boats to break off attacks when they came within 200–300nm of Britain. While valuable, it did not protect merchant ships in the mid-Atlantic. Once bases in France were established, U-boats could easily operate independently in waters immediately west of the escort limit.

Lorient was the first French port to receive a visit from a U-boat, when U-30 (the boat that sank *Athenia* and tangled with HMS *Ark Royal*'s aircraft) arrived on 7 July 1940 to take on provisions. Brest was open for business when a damaged U-65 stopped at the former French naval base on 22 August. The harbour facilities were not at full working capacity until 15 September, but U-65 could undergo repairs. It departed five days later.

In September St Nazaire, La Pallice and Bordeaux joined Brest and Lorient as U-boat bases. Initially German U-boats were stationed in the northern three harbours, while Italy operated its Atlantic submarines out of Bordeaux. Soon extensive facilities to service the U-boats, including bombproof reinforced concrete shelters, were being built in all five harbours.

The Kriegsmarine was joined by Italy's Regia Marina in September. Six Italian submarines arrived in Bordeaux that month, 12 more came in October, and the first war patrol left Bordeaux on 9 October. Eventually 32 Italian submarines would operate out of French ports.

Dönitz did not think highly of his Italian allies, a judgement somewhat justified by their performance. They sank only 106 ships, an average of 3⅓ ships per submarine, while suffering 50 per cent casualties. Dönitz had them operate in the latitudes between Cape Finisterre and Cape Verde.

When Britain occupied Iceland in May 1940, Coastal Command lacked aircraft for a squadron there. One arrived on 30 July, equipped with the Fairey Battle. A single-engine bomber, the Battle was better suited to infantry support than maritime patrol. (AC)

Dönitz moved his headquarters to Paris in September, closer to the theatre of operation. He moved still closer to his U-boats in November, to a château outside Lorient, after Hitler cancelled Operation *Sealion*, the invasion of Britain. Dönitz intended to use France as the main platform for the Battle of the Atlantic. German Baltic Sea U-boat bases would be used for training, while bases in Germany and Norway would facilitate U-boat movement to France. New U-boats joining the campaign reached French bases through an initial war patrol that started in Norway and swept north of Scotland into the North Atlantic.

The result was a slaughter in the mid-Atlantic, with 289 ships sunk between 1 June and 31 October, nearly two sinkings every day. The losses were limited by available U-boats rather than by British anti-submarine efforts. On 1 June there were only 48 U-boats in commission, including over a dozen being used for training. Twenty-four more would be commissioned between then and 31 October, but an additional five would be sunk. Excluding U-boats used as school boats to train new crews or those completing post-commissioning training, only 30 were available for war patrols at the end of October.

Coastal Command was evolving, too. Growth was slower than desired, but there was growth, after invasion fears cooled. Between September 1939 and October 1940, Coastal Command grew from 19 to 26 squadrons stationed in Britain and Ireland. Six of these were either fighter or strike squadrons, rather than maritime and anti-U-boat patrol. Additionally, there was a squadron operating out of Gibraltar, although this was made up of biplanes – Londons and Swordfish.

Coastal Command finally sent 98 Squadron to Iceland in July. It was equipped with Fairey Battles, a single-engine light bomber, designed for battlefield support, not maritime patrol. Operating out of a new airfield at Kaldadarnes, they offered air cover over the Atlantic waters immediately south of Iceland.

While these aircraft would have been useful if England was invaded, there were no maritime patrol squadrons available. Battles could operate in primitive airfields, and some feared the Germans might attempt a landing on Iceland. If that happened Battles could provide Commonwealth troops with air support. They could also carry four 250lb anti-submarine bombs on anti-submarine patrol, five times the bombload of Ansons.

The prevalence of night-time surface attacks by U-boats showed Coastal Command needed a night-time presence. During the first ten months of the war, Coastal Command was a daytime service. The Mk I ASV radar was finally in service during the summer of 1940, but was still in the development stage. The Mk II improved the ability to spot U-boats, but it required experienced operators to be effective. While first seeing service in July 1940, there were too few skilled radar operators. A final issue was the need to illuminate the target after it was spotted, a problem awaiting a solution during the summer of 1940. Radar remained a promise of future results.

Coastal Command aircraft were still spotting and attacking U-boats, making 31 sightings and attacks between June and August 1940. On 1 July a 10 Squadron Sunderland hit U-26 with several 250lb anti-submarine bombs. The damage prevented it from submerging, and its crew scuttled the boat after HMS *Gladiolus*, vectored by the Sunderland, appeared. It was the second U-boat sunk by Coastal Command, but the last to be sunk until more than a year later. U-boats moved their operations west and south in September. The number of U-boat sightings made by Coastal Command dropped by two thirds during the rest of the year. It was a frustrating period for Coastal Command.

## Dark winter: November 1940 to April 1941

The threat of a German invasion of England waned in September and October. By November, the Admiralty and Air Ministry could focus attention on problems other than the beaches of England's Channel coast. One such area was the Atlantic. The Battle of the Atlantic had seemed a controllable problem in May 1940, yet by November it had developed into a crisis.

In addition to the U-boats, a new threat menaced Britain's trade – the Fw 200 Condor. The Germans first stationed these aircraft in Bordeaux's Mérignac airport in June 1940. From there the aircraft could range far into the Atlantic, spot unescorted merchant ships and attack them. Since most merchant ships lacked anti-aircraft guns, they were helpless against the Condor.

An FW 200 lands at Mérignac airport in Bordeaux, France. Its improvised nature is illustrated by the off-centre bomb-bay under the fuselage. It sank well over 350,000 tons of shipping between June 1940 and February 1941. (AC)

Its first operational missions were flown in August. The first ship sunk was the 3,000-ton *Goathland*, sunk on 25 August steaming independently near Ireland. September and October saw a handful of sinkings by Fw 200s, all merchant vessels sailing independently. Condors sank six freighters in November and another six in December, still relatively low losses, but they sank 18 ships in January 1941, 25 in February and a dozen in March.

Condors only attacked unarmed ships sailing individually. While they flew individually, they flew outside the range of land-based fighters. Coastal Command attempted intercepting them as they flew past the south-west tip of Britain, but there was a lot of sky to search. Even when a Coastal Command fighter spotted a Condor, the fighter squadrons assigned to Coastal Command in 1940 and early 1941 flew Blenheims, and Condors could outrun Blenheims. The result of an encounter was a long stern chase, until the Condor escaped or the shorter-ranged Blenheim broke off due to fuel limitations.

The U-boat menace also remained. While the number of ships sunk each month dropped, U-boats sank over 100 merchant ships between November and January. In October the U-boats were joined by Italian submarines, which were less efficient than U-boats. Italian submarines in the Atlantic sank a total of 109 ships between October 1940 and the Italian surrender in September 1943 – a 36-month period. U-boats managed that total in three months during the winter of 1940–41. Yet the Italians still had to be countered.

More worrying was U-boats expanding their operations. They were not just moving west: they were moving south, operating off West Africa. This forced Britain to expand the convoy system, further thinning the escorts available for each convoy.

The Royal Navy's surface escort shortage eased when the United States agreed to swap 50 1,200-ton flush-deck destroyers to Britain in exchange for long-term leases on bases in the western Atlantic and British West Indies. The Destroyers for Bases Agreement was signed on 2 September 1940. Transfers began in October, but most destroyers needed work before reporting for escort duty, and only 30 were in service by May 1941.

A group photo of the flight personnel of 224 Squadron, the first Coastal Command squadron to fly one million miles of aerial reconnaissance missions. The photo was taken in recognition of this milestone. (AC)

The obvious answer was expanding Coastal Command. A shortage of available aircraft remained through to the end of 1940 and into February 1941. Coastal Command aircraft were needed in West Africa and as maritime patrol aircraft in Iceland. Yet Coastal Command received relatively few reinforcements beyond deliveries of previously contracted Sunderlands and Hudsons. Bomber Command temporarily transferred a second Whitley

Two U-boat captains at an awards ceremony in late 1940. Dönitz maintained morale through frequent recognition of outstanding performance. (AC)

squadron and a Wellington squadron to Coastal Command, and Fighter Command sent several Blenheim squadrons to Coastal Command, but that was it.

The good news was that the Whitleys and Wellingtons were outfitted with Mk II ASV radar. The bad news was while the radars could alert patrol aircraft to the presence of U-boats, no technique yet existed for conducting a radar-guided attack on a U-boat. U-boats disappeared into the radar scope's background clutter at aircraft attack ranges. There was no satisfactory means of spotting U-boats at night.

Aircraft and resources to reinforce Coastal Command were available. Bombers were rolling out of Britain's aircraft factories. Britain also received a windfall of new combat aircraft built in the United States following the fall of France, with aircraft ordered by France transferred to Britain. This included 120 four-engine Liberator bombers, 75 Martin Maryland twin-engine bombers, over 200 Douglas DB-7s (known in British service as the Havoc or Boston) and several hundred fighters (including 84 Grumman Martlets). These were all available by late 1940 and early 1941. (Once the aircraft originally contracted by France were delivered, additional aircraft were ordered by Britain, keeping these production lines open.)

All could have served as maritime patrol aircraft. The Wellington, still in production, had been used by Coastal Command. The Liberator had a range of 1800nm, while the Maryland and DB-7 could carry as much as the Hudson with ranges 10–20 per cent greater than the Hudson. Except, eventually, for 17 Liberators, none of these imports saw service in Coastal Command. They were routed to Bomber Command.

Similarly, Fighter Command assigned its worst twin-engine fighters to Coastal Command. Coastal Command received early-model Blenheims, while the new (and robust) Bristol Beaufighters were sent to Fighter Command during the first year of operational service. Fighter Command also received priority for airborne radar during this period, slowing its introduction in Coastal Command.

There were, however, promising developments. The Leigh Light was conceived during this period. The prototype was tested in March 1941, but it would not enter operational service for another year. The air-droppable 250lb depth charge entered service in January 1941, although it was not widely available until May. The first Hudsons of 269 Squadron arrived in Iceland in January 1941, replacing the Fairey Battles at Kaldadarnes. The entire squadron was there by April. Additionally, Coastal Command moved 95 Squadron, a Sunderland unit, to Sierra Leone to cover waters west of Africa. The move started in January 1941, but was not complete until March.

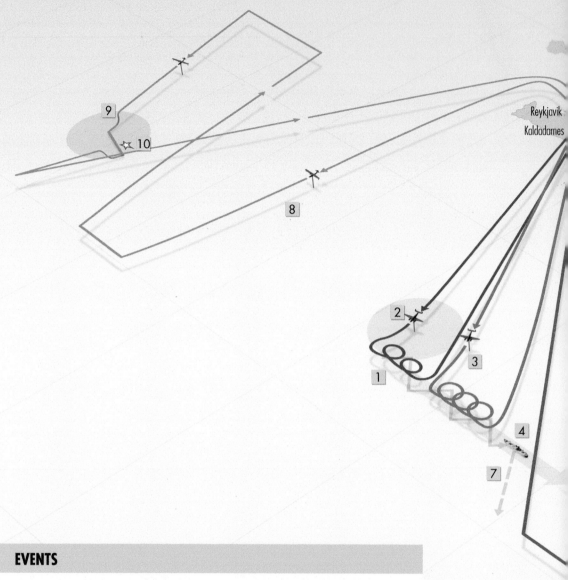

Reykjavik
Kaldadarnes

## EVENTS

1. Slow convoy passing near Iceland at 0700hrs.

2. A Hudson from Kaldadarnes is dispatched to escort the convoy – flies over the convoy for four hours watching for U-boats.

3. A new Hudson from Kaldadarnes relieves the first one, escorting the convoy.

4. The convoy after 12 hours of travel at 1900hrs.

5. A Kaldadarnes Hudson is sent on a patrol ahead of the convoy seeking U-boats in the path of the convoy.

6. It spots a U-boat, but the U-boat also spots the

Hudson and submerges before it can be attacked. The Hudson drops depth charges, and circles, but the U-boat does not resurface.

7. A warning is sent to the convoy, which changes course away from the spotted U-boat.

8. A Catalina from Reykjavik conducts a routine patrol west of Iceland.

9. The Catalina spots a surfaced U-boat, which does not spot it.

10. Catalina attacks the U-boat, damaging it – forcing it to submerge and return to France for repair.

# Iceland Patrol

Great Britain occupied Iceland in May 1940, but failed to base
significant aircraft there until spring 1941. By summer 1941, results
were evident – some as dramatic as the capture of U-570 by Iceland-
based aircraft. The real payoff was suppression of German U-boats
near Iceland, as shown in this graphic.

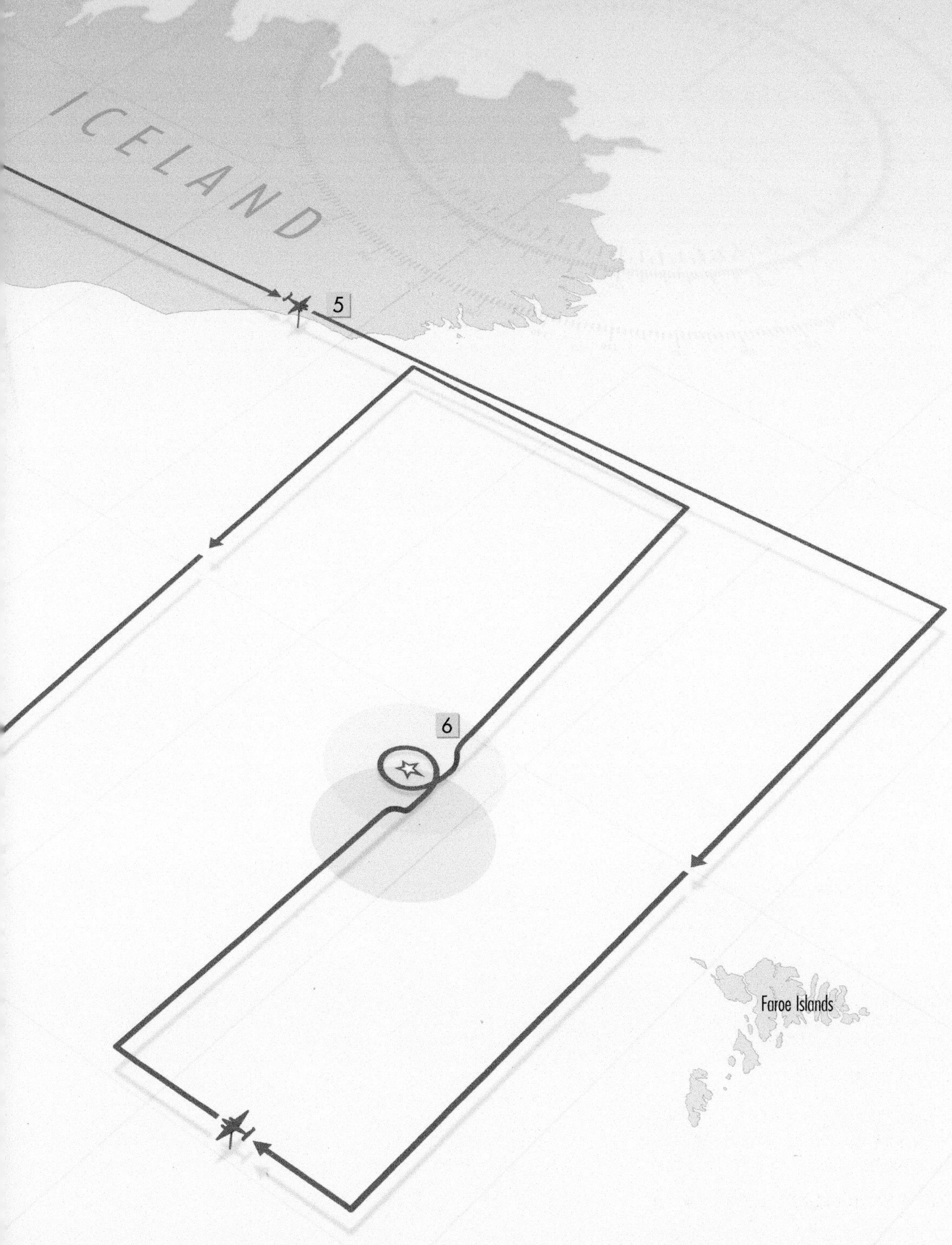

ICELAND

5

6

Faroe Islands

The Consolidated Catalina entered service with Coastal Command in the first quarter of 1941. With two engines, it was simpler to maintain than the Sunderland. Initially they were stationed in Gibraltar, Ireland and Iceland. (AC)

Overall, Dönitz was winning the Battle of the Atlantic. His U-boat captains called the period from July 1940 to March 1941 'the Happy Time'. An aggressive skipper would come back from a patrol with all torpedoes expended and between four and seven enemy ships sunk. U-99, commanded by Germany's most successful U-boat commander, Otto Kretchmer, sank 30 ships and damaged six others between June 1940 and March 1941. The only thing stopping Dönitz from winning his tonnage war was a lack of U-boats. More were being built, but were not yet available.

Britain took advantage of this shortage of U-boats and their signal intelligence to minimize losses during this period. Dönitz required U-boats to send in daily radio reports, and directed U-boats using coded messages. A combination of radio direction finding of U-boat transmissions and the British ability to read the Kriegsmarine's Enigma codes allowed the Admiralty to track U-boats in the Atlantic. Britain routed convoys away from U-boat concentrations. This cut losses, but reduced contact with U-boats, shrinking the opportunity to sink them. This allowed the U-boat fleet to increase its size.

Winston Churchill started World War II in charge of the Admiralty, becoming Prime Minister during the fall of France. By February 1941 he was concerned about the direction of the Battle of the Atlantic. On 6 March 1941 he expressed his concern, releasing a memo later known as the 'Battle of the Atlantic Directive'. It stated:

In view of various German statements, we must assume that the Battle of the Atlantic has begun. The next four months should enable us to defeat the attempt to strangle our food supplies and our connections with the United States. For this purpose –

1    We must take the offensive against the U-boat and the Fokke Wulf wherever we can and whenever we can. The U-boat at sea must be hunted, the U-boat in the building yard or in dock must be bombed. The Fokke Wulf, and other bombers employed against our shipping, must be attacked in the air and in their nests.

2    Extreme priority will be given to fitting out ships to catapult, or otherwise launch, fighter aircraft against bombers attacking our shipping. Proposals should be made within a week.

3    All the measures approved and now in train for the concentrations of the main strength of the Coastal Command upon the North-Western Approaches, and their assistance on the east coast by Fighter and Bomber Commands, will be pressed

forward. It may be hoped that, with the growing daylight and the new routes to be followed, the U-boat menace will soon be reduced. All the more important is it that the Fokke Wulf, and, if it comes, the Ju.88, should be effectively grappled with.

4     In view of the great need for larger numbers of escorting destroyers, it is for consideration whether the American destroyers now in service should go into dock for their second scale of improvements until the critical period of this new battle has been passed.

5     The Admiralty will re-examine, in conjunction with the Ministry of Shipping, the question of liberating from convoy ships between 13 and 12 knots, and also whether this might not be tried experimentally for a while.

6     The Admiralty will have the first claim on all the short-range AA guns, U.P. [Unrotated Projectile] weapons and P.A.C.s [Parachute and Cable – a rocket that launched a 400ft cable with parachutes at each end] that they can mount upon suitable merchant ships plying in the danger zone. Already 200 Bofors or their equivalents have been ordered to be made available by A.D.G.B. [Air Defence Great Britain] and the factories. But these should be followed by a constant flow of guns, together with crews, or nucleus crews, as and when they can be taken over by the Admiralty. A programme for three months should be made.

The memo reprioritized Britain's war effort. Coastal Command would nearly double over the next six months, growing from 26 squadrons to 46. The maritime patrol squadrons, used to hunt U-boats, rose from 20 to 33. This allowed Coastal Command to form a fourth operational group, 19 Group, which took over responsibility for what had been the southern part of 15 Group's territory, the Atlantic south and west of Northern Ireland. Coastal Command also began aerial patrols of the Bay of Biscay, attempting to intercept U-boats as they left their home ports for an Atlantic mission or returned to them after its conclusion.

The Lerwick was finally gone, while the Anson was retired from anti-submarine warfare service, replaced by more capable aircraft. The first Catalina squadron became operational in April. More importantly, Coastal Command managed to pry the first 17 Liberators delivered away from Bomber Command. This was enough to form one VLR (Very Long Range) patrol squadron.

Moreover, the Royal Navy's luck seemed to change. March saw the Royal Navy sink five U-boats, three commanded by the Kriegsmarine's three leading U-boat aces: U-47 (Gunter Prien), U-99 (Otto Kretchmer) and U-100 (Joachim Schepke). Kretchmer was captured, while Prien and Schepke – and all hands aboard U-47 and U-100 – died. Since Dönitz had only 25 operational boats in the Atlantic, this reduced U-boat strength by 20 per cent. U-boats sank 41 ships and Condors ten more in April, but although British losses rose in May and June, 'the Happy Time' was ending.

## Neutrality patrol: May 1941 to September 1941

A change in policy often takes time to implement. The 'Battle of the Atlantic Directive' finally began showing results in May 1941, when the 250lb depth charge started reaching Coastal Command in large numbers. This gave Coastal Command an effective weapon against U-boats. It took time to learn how to best use this weapon – it was August before a Coastal Command aircraft sank a U-boat with one – but for the first time since the war began, Coastal Command had a U-boat-killing weapon that all of its aircraft could use. The Anson, which could not, was being phased out.

The aircraft spigot was finally being opened wider, and Coastal Command began adding aircraft and squadrons, slowly at first, but more quickly as time went on. The first Catalina squadrons were in service by May, and one played a role in tracking down the German battleship *Bismarck* during its breakout in May 1941. The Catalina had a longer range than the Sunderland, could carry a larger bombload and had only two engines, simplifying maintenance. Catalinas were soon stationed in Iceland, Gibraltar and Northern Ireland.

Iceland was open for business by May 1941. A refuelling port was established in Reykjavik, allowing British destroyers and escort vessels to extend coverage to convoys in the mid-Atlantic. In addition to the land-plane airbase in Kaldadarnes, both an airfield and a seaplane base were opened at Reykjavik. More Coastal Command squadrons were moved to Iceland, including 330 Squadron, equipped with Northrop N-3PB Nomads, a single-engine floatplane ordered by Norway in late 1939. The 24-plane order was transferred to Britain after Germany conquered Norway. In turn, Britain assigned the aircraft to a squadron of Norwegian pilots flying with the RAF after Norway's fall.

Coastal Command also saw its first change-of-command since the war began, with Sir Philip Joubert de la Ferté relieving Bowhill. It was Joubert de la Ferté's second tour with Coastal Command. He had been briefly in charge of Coastal Command in 1936–37 before taking command of RAF Forces in India. Bowhill moved to a posting with Ferry Command and later Transport Command. In Ferry Command, his Coastal Command experience aided in flying aircraft over the Atlantic. This eliminated the need to ship aircraft, including the Hudson, by freighters, speeding delivery time.

Britain had also gained an ally, albeit one that was officially a neutral power. The United States, alarmed by German expansion and the French defeat, wanted Germany contained. Once convinced that Britain intended to fight on, United States President Franklin D. Roosevelt determined to help Britain and provide it with 'all aid short of war'. The destroyers for bases swap was one example. In March 1941 the US Congress passed the Lend-Lease Act, permitting the United States to provide Britain with material assistance.

In April 1941 the United States accepted an invitation by the Danish Government-in-Exile to serve as the protector of Greenland. The United States built weather stations and airfields

The navigator of a Hudson passes a course change to the pilot. Hudsons began patrolling Icelandic waters in 1941. Maritime patrol required tedious hours flying over featureless ocean, demanding accurate navigation. (AC)

in Greenland, with an eye towards anti-submarine operations. A week later, Admiral Earnest King, then commanding the US Atlantic Fleet, ordered US Navy forces that any belligerent aircraft or warship which approached within 25 miles of Western Hemisphere land masses be treated as intending to attack. The only exceptions were powers with West Indies Colonies, so British, French, Danish or Dutch forces could pass near Western Hemisphere soil, but German and Italian forces could not.

This one-sided 'neutrality' was extended on 27 May, following the *Bismarck*'s breakout and sinking. Roosevelt proclaimed an unlimited national emergency, putting the US military at a state of readiness 'to repel any and all acts or threats of aggression directed toward any part of the Western Hemisphere'. This put the United States on a war footing within a declared neutrality zone. The US Navy created a Neutrality Patrol to enforce neutrality west of the boundary.

On 16 June Britain asked the United States to occupy Iceland so Britain could redeploy its ground forces that were in Iceland elsewhere. The US cajoled Iceland's government into requesting US protection. The defence of Iceland was transferred to the United States on 7 July, and the next day it occupied the country with a US Marine Corps brigade. US Army troops reinforced, and eventually replaced, the Marines in August, reinforced by two US Navy patrol squadrons: VP-73 flying Catalinas and VP-74 flying Mariners. The Coastal Command remained, and British and US troops co-existed in Iceland into 1942.

Further straining neutrality, the United States agreed to escort convoys as far east as Iceland on 9 August, then carried things one step further following the *Greer* Incident. On 4 September, after a Coastal Command Hudson dropped depth charges on U-652 west of Iceland, the U-boat assumed the nearby US Navy destroyer *Greer* was the attacker. The U-boat responded by firing torpedoes at *Greer*, which retaliated by depth-charging U-652. On 11 September Roosevelt stated that U-boats entered the neutrality zone at their own risk, and ordered US warships to attack any U-boat threatening convoys escorted by US warships.

This brought the United States into a de facto belligerent status, west of Iceland. Dönitz wanted permission for U-boats to attack US warships, but this was denied. Hitler had

In July 1941, at the invitation of Britain and Iceland, the United States occupied the island, assuming responsibility for its defence. This shows US Marines landing at Reykjavik in landing craft. (AC)

Coastal Command scored its first clear kill on 25 August 1941 when a Catalina from 209 Squadron bracketed U-452 with a pair of 450lb depth charges. Although an armed trawler assisted, U-452 was probably fatally damaged by the Catalina. (AC)

invaded Russia on 22 June and was fighting a major land war there. In the summer of 1941 Hitler wanted to avoid the complications which would result if the United States became a full and active belligerent. He ordered US Navy warships to be left alone, although several, including the destroyers *Kearney* and *Reuben James* and fleet oiler *Salinas*, were torpedoed, likely in the belief they were British or by torpedoes aimed at other ships in their convoys. Both sides continued to pretend the United States was neutral, a charade maintained until Japan attacked Pearl Harbor.

The net result of American intervention was that, for the first time in the war, Coastal Command's burdens were eased. Not by much, but any relief was noticeable. Additionally, by midsummer, convoys continued from one end of the Atlantic to the other. British warships were now escorting convoys between Iceland and Britain (refuelling at Iceland), while Canadian and US warships protected convoys west of Iceland.

The presence of Coastal Command squadrons in Iceland had a near-immediate effect. Combined with Sunderland and Catalina flying boats operating out of Lough Erne (a flying boat station on a freshwater lake in Northern Ireland) and the Liberator squadron at Nutts Corner, near Belfast, air cover was now available over the entire length of the northern convoy route between Iceland and Britain. An air gap still existed west of Iceland and south of Greenland, but it was then at the extreme operational range limit of the Type VII U-boats. Resupply at sea from 'milch cow' supply U-boats would change this, but that was a year off. Daylight surface operations for U-boats near Iceland became risky, as Hudsons from 269 Squadron and Catalinas from 209 Squadron patrolled the waters around Iceland.

How risky Icelandic waters had become for U-boats was demonstrated in August. On 25 August a Catalina from 209 Squadron caught U-452, on the sixth day of its first war patrol, cruising on the surface. Using new tactical instructions issued just one month earlier, the Catalina dropped four 450lb depth charges on the submarine, set to shallow depth. They landed around the submerging U-boat and blew it back to the surface. The Catalina then strafed the U-boat, until an anti-submarine trawler, HMS *Vascama*, attracted by the commotion joined the fight. U-452 submerged again, but *Vascama* dropped a string of depth-charges on the U-boat, sinking it.

Less than two days later, the Hudsons of 269 Squadron accomplished something even more remarkable and never repeated during the war: they captured a U-boat unassisted by surface ships. U-570 was on its first war patrol. It surfaced at 1050hrs, just as a patrolling Hudson was overhead and attacked it with depth charges. The attack was ferociously noisy, but did not seriously damage U-570. Its crew was green and seasick, however, and its captain, Hans-Joachim Rahmlow, inexperienced. Both now panicked. Convinced the forward part of the ship was filling with chlorine gas, from seawater mixing with battery acid, the crew sealed off the bow and the captain ordered the ship to surface and be abandoned. The crew quickly crowded onto the deck and conning tower.

Unwilling to plunge into the freezing Icelandic water, and being strafed by the Hudson which originally attacked it, U-570 surrendered, the crew waving white shirts and boards. The pilot of the Hudson ceased fire, calling other aircraft to join him. These included the Catalina which sank U-452 two days earlier. U-570's skipper sent out an uncoded radio message for help, and had the U-boat's secret equipment pitched overboard. This included the Enigma code machine.

In response to this radio call, U-boats and surface ships rushed to the scene. The swarm of aircraft kept the U-boats away, and an armed trawler arrived at 2200hrs, near sunset, and took possession of the prize. Despite an attack by a Norwegian-manned Northrup unaware it had been surrendered the next morning, the British managed to bring U-570 safely to Reykjavik.

While the secret papers and Enigma machine were gone, U-570 proved an intelligence bonanza, providing a wealth of information about the Type VII submarine. Nor was the destruction of its Enigma machine a loss. Britain already had one, taken from U-110, captured by surface warships. U-110's crew was unaware the Enigma machine had been seized, the boat having sunk under tow to Iceland after its secret equipment had been removed.

U-570's capture could not be concealed, so having its skipper radio its code equipment had been destroyed kept the Germans from realizing their Enigma code had been cracked

# Capture of the U-570

The crew of the U-570 was having a bad day on 27 August 1941. The U-boat was three days out of Trondheim on its first cruise. Everything was going wrong. The air compressor was malfunctioning. The diesels were not tuned, causing unpleasant vibrations. The hydrophones (passive listening gear) had been knocked out after U-570 bottomed out heading to Trondheim. Plus the crew was seasick. A seasick sailor in a crowded U-boat, vomiting into buckets around your close-packed crewmates, was a good way to get everyone else seasick.

The U-boat's skipper, Hans Rahmlow, took the boat to the surface that morning seeking a convoy (because the hydrophones were out). He no sooner surfaced than U-570 was attacked by a Hudson from 269 Squadron out of Kaldadarnes. The Hudson spotted U-570 on its ASV radar and immediately attacked.

U-570 neglected to search for aircraft before surfacing. Rahmlow's first warning was the sound of aircraft engines when he opened the bridge hatch. He slammed the hatch shut, ordering a dive. Of the four 250lb depth charges dropped, two bracketed U-570's bow. The boat was shaken and plunged into darkness, the electric motors were knocked out and the crew panicked. Believing salt water had gotten into the batteries, generating chlorine gas, Rahmlow surfaced, ordering the crew to abandon ship.

With the sea cold enough to freeze anyone in it within hours, no one wanted to jump in. The Hudson, still there, began strafing U-570. Unwilling to scuttle and unable to dive, the crew surrendered by waving white shirts. Since the Hudson had no more depth charges, its captain, James Thompson, accepted the surrender. Having hours of fuel left, he remained at the scene.

Another Hudson (armed with depth charges) soon arrived, ready to sink U-570 if it did not surrender. They were eventually joined by a Catalina from 209 Squadron. This plate shows the scene at that point, with two Hudsons circling and the Catalina rushing to join them. They would circle for another eight hours until the trawler *Northern King* arrived to take possession of U-570. It was the second U-boat captured by the Royal Navy, and the first and only U-boat captured solely by aircraft.

## OPPOSITE BAY OF BISCAY PATROLS

The Bay of Biscay served as a funnel for all U-boats departing from or heading toward French ports. A distant blockade of these ports, by using long-range Coastal Command aircraft outside German fighter coverage range offered obvious advantages. Even if the aircraft did not sink U-boats transiting the Bay, they forced the U-boats to submerge, slowing their passage considerably and shortening the time the U-boats would spend on patrol. Brest, because it was close to Britain, was relatively easy to blockade, since it was within reach of aircraft such as the Hudson. But in 1941 only Sunderlands, Catalinas and Liberators had the range to completely patrol the Bay, and there were too few available for an ironclad blockade.

and the British were reading it. Eventually, after operation testing ended, U-570 was commissioned into the Royal Navy as HMS Graph, spending the rest of its active career hunting U-boats.

Those were the only two U-boats Coastal Command sank during this period. Yet the sinking underscored the effectiveness of ASV combined with new bombing tactics. The density of U-boats patrolling waters off Gibraltar or the west coast of Africa was low, and the total number of Coastal Command aircraft were few. Encounters were still rare. Coastal Command aircraft near Africa also had to contend with Vichy France fighters, which sought out and attacked British aircraft.

Yet Dönitz was not yet worrying about Coastal Command. U-boat production – or rather its lack – was his major concern as he struggled to keep their numbers up. By the middle of 1941 production was finally gearing up, with U-boats coming off the building ways in significant numbers. Germany built 63 U-boats between 1935 and the end of 1939. It almost doubled that total in 1940, building another 50. However, Germany lost 31 U-boats by the end of 1940, and had withdrawn 41 surviving Type II U-boats from active service in the Atlantic.

By January 1941 Dönitz had fewer boats available for war patrols than he had in September 1939. By May 1941 the new construction was becoming available, and the number of U-boats on patrol soared. May started with 24 U-boats on patrol, the daily average that month, and three times the average number of U-boats on patrol each day in January. The monthly daily average continued to rise until August, when there was an

Two days later, on 27 August, Hudsons from 269 Squadron forced U-570 to surrender after initially damaging it with depth charges. U-570 was successfully towed to Reykjavik and is shown here, entering the harbour. (AC)

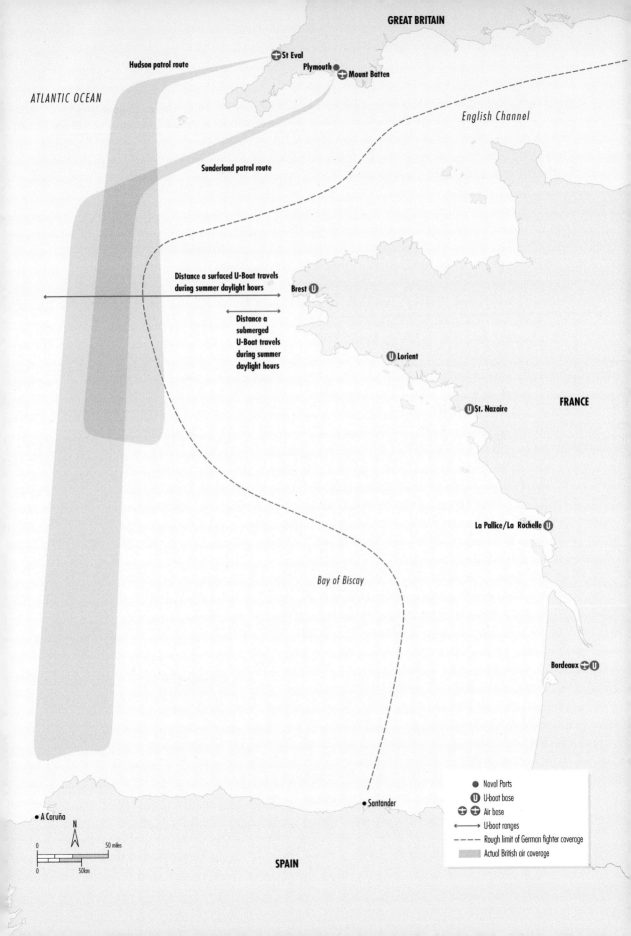

GREAT BRITAIN

St Eval

Plymouth ● Mount Batten

Hudson patrol route

ATLANTIC OCEAN

English Channel

Sunderland patrol route

Distance a surfaced U-Boat travels
during summer daylight hours

Brest Ⓤ

Distance a
submerged
U-Boat travels
during summer
daylight hours

Ⓤ Lorient

Ⓤ St. Nazaire

FRANCE

La Pallice/La Rochelle Ⓤ

Bay of Biscay

Bordeaux Ⓤ

Santander

● A Coruña

N

0        50 miles

0      50km

SPAIN

| | |
|---|---|
| ● | Naval Ports |
| Ⓤ | U-boat base |
| ⊕ ⊕ | Air base |
| ←——→ | U-boat ranges |
| - - - - | Rough limit of German fighter coverage |
| � | Actual British air coverage |

average of 41 U-boats on patrol in Atlantic waters. There were as many as 50 U-boats in the Atlantic between the start of May and the end of August, and no fewer than 21. The numbers then began dipping in September as a trickle of U-boats began relocating to the Mediterranean. During the summer months of 1941, from June until September, Atlantic U-boats sank 223 ships – over 1.15 million tons. This was close to the totals needed to win the tonnage war.

### Enter the escort carrier: October to December 1941

The last three months of 1941 brought a new phase to the Battle of the Atlantic, one that saw both sides mature into formidable fighting forces which shook off early-war ineffectiveness. For the British, the most profound change was not the continued growth and increasing effectiveness of Coastal Command, although that remained crucial. Rather it was the re-entry of the Fleet Air Arm into the fight against the U-boat.

Between October 1939 and October 1941, the FAA had been largely on the sidelines of the Battle of the Atlantic. It had been busy elsewhere, supporting Royal Navy operations in Norway and the Mediterranean over those two years, including an air raid against the Italian Navy in Taranto harbour that sank or heavily damaged three Italian battleships. It even sank U-64 in April 1940, bombing it in Herjangsfjord during the fight for Norway. But that had been done in support of Fleet activities against German surface forces in Herjangsfjord, part of a larger effort supporting a surface ship attack.

Lack of aircraft and trained aircrew meant the Royal Navy was hard-pressed to keep even one aircraft carrier staffed to full capability. The loss of HMS *Courageous* and near-loss of HMS *Ark Royal* discouraged the use of fleet carriers for anti-U-boat hunter-killer teams. The 'Battle of the Atlantic Directive' then refocused attention on using carrier aircraft against U-boats, calling for the installation of catapults on merchant ships to permit them to carry fighters capable of attacking Fw 200s.

These catapult-launched aircraft were (literally) one-shot deals. The fighters used could not land on the merchantman, which lacked a flight deck. Once launched, the aircraft had to be ditched when it ran out of fuel or flown to shore. Britain eventually had 59 such CAM (Catapult Armed Merchantman) ships, which destroyed nine enemy aircraft. An alternative was an escort carrier, a fast liner converted to a flight-deck warship, or even adding a flight deck to a bulk carrier, which allowed the aircraft to land.

An escort carrier had another advantage over the CAM ship. Since the aircraft could land, they could conduct different types of missions as well as multiple missions. They could fly anti-submarine reconnaissance, scouting out U-boats in advance of the convoy. They could also attack U-boats. A fighter's machine guns could do damage, or the carrier could include aircraft like the Swordfish, which could bomb U-boats. There were even weapons with which Swordfish could sink U-boats by 1941, as they could carry four 250lb depth charges, enough for an effective attack.

HMS *Audacity* was Britain's first escort carrier. Without a hangar deck, it kept its aircraft on the flight deck. It accompanied only four convoys before being sunk, but proved the value of escort carriers for protecting convoys. (USNHHC)

A pilot exits a Fleet Air Arm Martlet, the British version of the Grumman F4F Wildcat. HMS *Audacity* carried these, and they proved useful for both driving away the FW 200 and scouting for and attacking U-boats. (AC)

In January 1941 the Royal Navy finally decided escort carriers were an experiment worth trying. The Royal Navy took an ocean boarding vessel, *Empire Audacity*, and sent it to Blyth for conversion into an aircraft carrier. The ship began life as the 12,000 ton German liner *Hannover*. Trapped in the neutral Dutch port of Curaçao when the war began, *Hannover* was captured in the Caribbean when attempting a run to Germany in March 1940. The shipyard chosen for the conversion had built the world's first aircraft carrier, the seaplane carrier HMS *Ark Royal* in 1914.

The conversion was completed in June, and the ship commissioned on 17 June. The conversion was so hasty that there was no hangar deck, only a flight deck. Its aircraft were stowed on the flight deck. After a brief period for acceptance trials and air group training, it entered active service in September. Its career would be just over three months, but it would change the Battle of the Atlantic.

Yet another use of FAA aircraft occurred during this period; the dedicated use of Swordfish for anti-submarine patrol around Gibraltar. Three Swordfish squadrons were effectively stranded in Gibraltar following the sinking of aircraft carriers HMS *Ark Royal* and HMS *Eagle*. Some were fitted with Mk III ASV, and patrolled the waters around Gibraltar.

This measure turned the Mediterranean into a U-boat trap. A strong current ran from the Atlantic to the Mediterranean, facilitating submerged U-boats entering the Mediterranean but preventing them from exiting. The only way to leave was to travel on the surface. Surfaced submarines could evade surface ships during a night run into the Atlantic: Italian submarines slipped out of the Mediterranean in their dozens between September 1940 and May 1941. But patrolling Swordfish stopped that. They could attack U-boats or vector British warships to surfaced submarines. Only one Italian submarine succeeded in exiting the Mediterranean after radar-equipped Swordfish began guarding the straits.

Another positive sign for the British was the maturity of airborne radar. On 30 November a Whitley from 502 Squadron patrolling the Bay of Biscay spotted U-30 on its Mk II ASV

## EVENTS

1. 813 Squadron (FAA) Swordfish 'A' departs Gibraltar

2. Conducts a radar-assisted search of the Atlantic approaches to the Straits of Gibraltar.

3. Radar makes contact with U-451, cruising surfaced on the African Coast, Swordfish dives to attack.

4. Swordfish drops flare to illuminate U-boat.

5. U-boat dives, Swordfish drops 3 250lb depth charges set at 50ft. Attracted by the flares corvette HMS *Myosotis* investigates, finds an oil slick and one survivor – the officer of the watch on deck when the submarine dived.

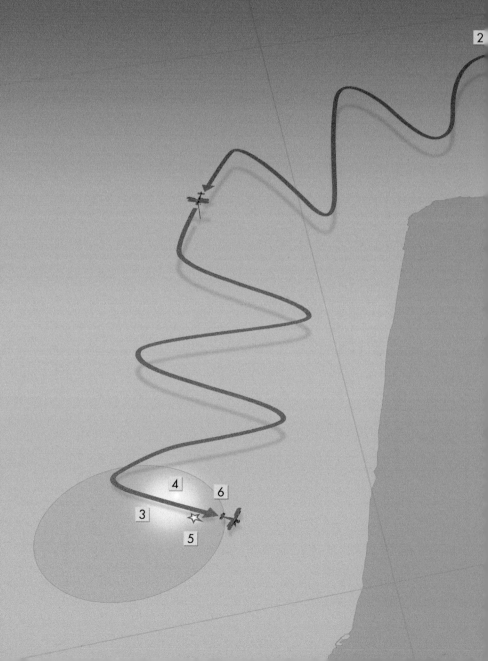

1

TANGIER

# The Death of U-451

The Mediterranean Sea trapped German U-boats. A strong current in the Straits of Gibraltar made exiting the Mediterranean submerged impossible. Radar-equipped British aircraft guarded the Straits, making a surfaced passage perilous. On December 21, 1941, *U-451* learned how effective Gibraltar-based British ASW aircraft were. It became the first U-boat sunk by aerial radar-guided night-time attack.

and made a successful radar-guided attack. It was credited with sinking U-206. In reality, it only damaged the U-boat, which was actually U-71. It was the first successful radar attack on a U-boat. On 21 December a Swordfish from 812 Squadron made a successful night-time attack on U-451, the first time a U-boat was sunk by radar guidance at night.

The arrival and growth of VLR Coastal Command patrol squadrons was another boon. These used four-engine bombers built in the United States, typically Liberators, but also including the B-17 Flying Fortress, which entered the RAF's inventory as the Fortress. Long range aircraft, Liberators were unsuitable for Bomber Command's German bombing offensive. Bomber Command reluctantly released 17 Liberators to Coastal Command, which were formed into 120 Squadron operating out of Northern Ireland.

From there they could cover much of the North Atlantic, as far south as Bordeaux and as far west as Iceland. The effect was felt immediately. Wolf-pack attacks dropped wherever the Liberators flew. The Liberators were not yet sinking U-boats, but they were spotting U-boats near convoys, allowing the convoys to evade the tracking boats and convoy escorts to hunt out potential threats. The Liberators could also shoot down or drive off prowling Condors. In late November, 220 Squadron, which had transitioned to Fortresses, joined 120 Squadron at Nutts Corner.

As for Dönitz, U-boats continued to be commissioned in greater numbers. Production continued unabated, and was accelerating. Although growth was good, staffing the new constructions became difficult. It took a capable officer to successfully command a U-boat, someone bold enough to take reasonable chances, cautious enough to avoid unnecessary risks and experienced enough to know the difference between the two. There were too few of those officers available. The pool of men able to serve as capable petty officers, the backbone of any navy, but especially a submarine, was also too shallow.

The loss of U-570 illustrated what happened with an ill-trained crew and inexperienced captain. The growth rate of the U-boat service forced Dönitz to throw crews into the Battle of the Atlantic and hope they could gain enough experience on their first patrols to survive later ones. Performance dropped over the next quarter. From October to December only 66 ships were sunk for over 340,000 tons. Nearly half were sunk in one month, October, with a precipitous drop in November.

There were two reasons for this drop. The first was known to Dönitz, as he was being forced to transfer U-boats to the Mediterranean. The war there increased in intensity during 1941, with Germany invading the Balkans and sending troops to assist Italy in North Africa. Italy began withdrawing Atlantic-based submarines in July. By October, over a third of its surviving submarines returned to Italy. In September Hitler had Dönitz reinforce the Italians with U-boats, even though there were fewer merchant targets in the Mediterranean. Four departed at the end of September, joined by another 22 by the end of 1941. This reduced the boats available to patrol in Atlantic waters.

A second reason for the reduction in shipping sunk was unknown to Dönitz. The British were by now reading Dönitz's signals, having cracked the Enigma code used by the Germans. With fewer U-boats in the Atlantic, Dönitz could not be strong everywhere. The Royal Navy was able to route convoys away from known U-boat concentrations. While Dönitz felt reason to feel confident, the Royal Navy was beginning to contain the U-boat and Condor threats in the last quarter of 1941.

This was shown most clearly in operations involving the carrier HMS *Audacity*. It escorted four convoys before it was sunk: OG 74 (Britain to Gibraltar) which left the Clyde on 12 September, HG 74 (Gibraltar to Britain) which sailed on 2 October, OG 76 which left Britain on 28 October and HG 76 which departed Gibraltar on 14 December.

The carrier only had fighters aboard, Grumman Martlets, aircraft originally intended for France but sold to Britain. The stubby Grumman fighters were there to protect convoys from Condors, a role in which they excelled. On the first three convoys the Martlets shot down

five Condors and chased off others. Condors sank one ship and U-boats sank five ships in Convoy OG-74, but Martlets protected HG-74 from numerous Condor attacks.

It was HG-76, the final convoy escorted by *Audacity*, that showed how valuable carrier escorts could be. A long-running series of clashes, lasting over a week, resulted in the loss of two escorts (including *Audacity*) two freighters, one Condor and five U-boats.

As HG-76 left Gibraltar on 14 December, in addition to *Audacity*, the escort consisted of 17 warships, including Escort Group-36 under the command of Captain Frederic 'Jonnie' Walker, Britain's deadliest U-boat killer. German observers in Spain reported the convoy's departure. Dönitz formed an eight-boat wolf pack, named *Seerauber*, to intercept the convoy. Condors were also sent in search of it.

First blood was drawn by the Allies. On 15 December, just a day into the voyage, a Gibraltar-based Sunderland spotted U-131 heading for its position in the search line. The Sunderland was unable to attack, but directed the Australian destroyer *Nestor* to U-131's vicinity. *Nestor* found the U-boat with an ASDIC search, and sank it with depth charges.

The convoy made a turn south after leaving Gibraltar to avoid the U-boat picket line. It went unspotted until the morning of 16 December, when a searching Condor found the convoy. It took until midday for the U-boats to make contact, but they were driven off by the escorts. The next morning two Martlets spotted U-131 and strafed it, directing surface escorts to the U-boat. One Martlet was downed, but three destroyers sank U-131.

That night, 17 December, the Germans again attacked the convoy, but were once more driven off by the surface escorts, with U-434 being sunk in the pre-dawn hours of 18 December. *Audacity* then spotted incoming aircraft on its radar that morning, and scrambled two Martlets which drove off the Condors. Two more Condors came snooping at 1430hrs: this time one Condor was shot down and the other driven away by the Martlets.

Consolidated Liberators under construction for Britain in late 1940 or early 1941. Coastal Command received only 17 of the first 120 made, just enough to equip 120 Squadron, which significantly reduced U-boat effectiveness in their patrol area. (AC)

## OPPOSITE THE PROGRESS OF CONVOY HG-76

HG-76 was the fourth convoy protected by the Royal Navy's first escort carrier, *Audacity*. Its departure from Gibraltar was reported by German spies in Spain, and Donitz made a major effort to attack the convoy. The result was a week-long brawl which saw the loss of two of the convoy's cargo ships, one escorting destroyer, *Audacity*, and six U-boats. It was the first major convoy battle where the Germans lost more U-boats than the British lost ship, a change largely due to the almost-continuous air escort available.

At dusk *Seerauber*'s U-boats made another concerted attempt on the convoy, finally drawing blood. At 0400hrs on 19 December, U-574 torpedoed and sank the destroyer HMS *Stanley*. The U-boat in turn was rammed and sunk by Walker's flagship, the sloop *Stork*. Shortly afterwards, U-108 torpedoed and sank the 2,869-ton *Ruckinge*, the first freighter lost by the convoy.

At 0730hrs on 19 December, another Condor came snooping, only to be sent packing by a Martlet. In the afternoon, patrolling Martlets spotted two surfaced U-boats. Convoy HG-76 made a radical turn, breaking contact with *Seerauber*. Dönitz sent more U-boats after the convoy but the wolf pack was unable to attack until the night of 21/22 December. After nightfall, *Audacity* left the convoy. At 2033hrs a freighter, the 3,324-ton *Annavore*, was torpedoed and sunk by U-567, commanded by U-boat ace Engelbert Endrass. It was his last kill, as the sloop HMS *Deptford* found and sank U-567.

Responding to the attack, the convoy filled the sky with snowflake flares, to illuminate the surface of the sea. U-751 spotted the solitary *Audacity* silhouetted against this light and fired a spread of torpedoes at it. Two struck home, and the carrier went down with 73 of its crew.

The next morning HG-76 was within range of Nutts Corner-based Liberators. The first one arrived over the convoy a little before 1100hrs, its first act being to chase away a shadowing Condor. Two hours later the Liberator attacked and drove off a U-boat attempting to stalk HG-76. A second Liberator relieved the first in mid-afternoon. Before dark this aircraft attacked three more U-boats. While it sank none of them, all three were forced to submerge and lost contact with HG-76. The next day the convoy was under continuous daytime escort. Dönitz finally ordered the attacks discontinued, and HG-76 arrived at the Clyde without additional incident.

On 21 December 1941 a radar-equipped Swordfish spotted U-451 with its ASV radar. Illuminating the U-boat with flares, it sank U-542 with depth charges. The first time an aircraft sank a U-boat at night, it would not be the last. (AC)

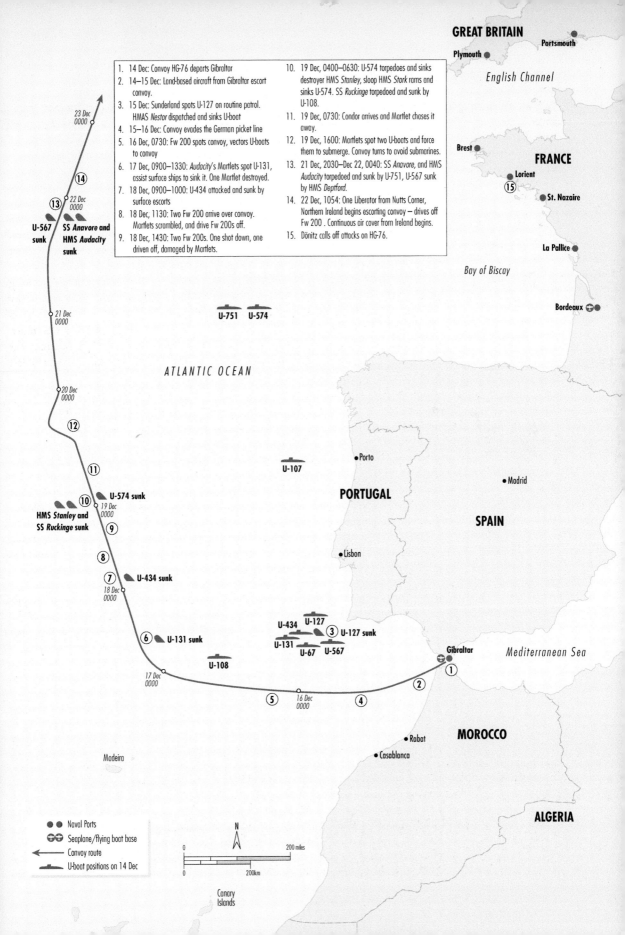

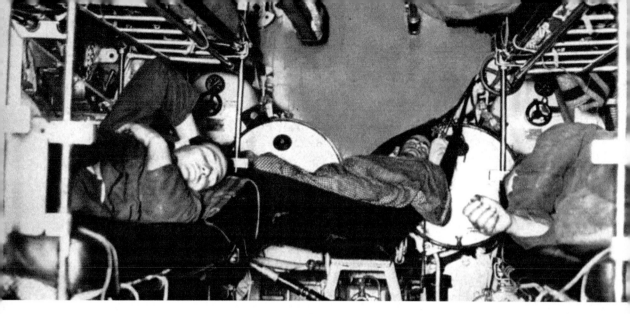

# AFTERMATH AND ANALYSIS

Life aboard a U-boat was crowded. Here part of the off-duty watch sleeps in the forward torpedo room. They have extra space because the spare torpedoes they share space with are gone, likely having been expended. (AC)

Despite the loss of *Audacity*, the battle for HG-76 was the first clear-cut Allied victory in a convoy battle during World War II. It was the first time more U-boats were sunk than ships in a convoy, illustrating the power of an escort carrier teamed with a good escort group.

A U-boat loss perhaps more significant than those lost during the battle for Convoy HG-76 occurred the same day as *Audacious* sank. Off the coast of Africa, a radar-equipped Swordfish spotted U-451 at night with its radar and then proceeded to sink it. It was the first time a U-boat was sunk at night by a radar-equipped aircraft.

U-boat losses were heavy in the closing month of 1941. Germany lost ten U-boats in December, and had lost five in November. These 15 were nearly half the total of 35 U-boats lost in 1941. Radar, VLR aircraft and escort carriers had dramatically demonstrated their worth during the last three months of 1941. It appeared Britain, particularly Coastal Command and the Fleet Air Arm, was finally getting the U-boat menace under control.

In many ways late 1941 was analogous to the situation in early spring in 1940, when Britain seemed to be coping with the U-boat problem. Had the battlefield remained constant or grown incrementally as it had through most of 1941, Britain could possibly have quashed the U-boats by July 1942. However, as in June 1940, the battlefield grew dramatically in 1942.

On 7 December 1941 the Empire of Japan attacked US forces in the Pacific. This included the attack on the US fleet at Pearl Harbor, but the Japanese also attacked the Philippines, Guam and Wake Island, invading all three by the end of December. The Japanese offensive included possessions controlled by Britain, the Netherlands, France and independent Commonwealth nations, such as Australia and New Zealand. Britain's resources suddenly had to be spread across a much wider war.

The United States was also drawn into the war in Europe. It had effectively been at war with Germany and its allies since it assumed the defence of Iceland in July 1941. Since July the conflict between Germany and the United States had escalated. On 4 September the US destroyer *Greer* and U-562 exchanged fire, trading torpedoes and depth charges.

The destroyer *Kearney* and fleet oiler *Salinas* were torpedoed in October. Both survived. On 31 October the US destroyer *Reuben James* was torpedoed and sunk west of Iceland.

Roosevelt issued a directive to shoot U-boats on sight after the *Greer* Incident. *Reuben James* was escorting a convoy heading to Britain, the act of a belligerent, not a neutral. Yet the US and Germany both pretended they were still at peace. Even after the sinking of the *Reuben James*, Roosevelt lacked the domestic support to declare war on Germany, and Hitler did not want the undivided attention and resources of the United States used against Germany.

The Japanese attacks, made without consulting Germany, changed Hitler's calculations. The Tripartite Pact Germany and Italy had signed with Japan in September 1940 was a defensive alliance. Germany could have remained neutral. Yet Hitler chose to declare war on the United States on 11 December, a declaration reciprocated by the US later the same day.

It is understandable why Hitler chose this course. He lost patience with the pretence the two nations were not at war. The humiliations inflicted on the United States by Japan in the Pacific led Hitler to underestimate United States military capabilities. In the long run, he would have been wiser to forgo going to war with the United States.

Without a German declaration of war, Roosevelt would have found it difficult to declare war on Germany in 1941. The attention of United States voters was firmly fixed on Japan: the public wanted revenge against the aggressors. If the United States maintained neutrality with Germany, Britain would likely have been denied badly needed US resources. Even Lend-Lease aid might have been funnelled to fight the United States' Pacific War.

Hitler's decision gave Britain a major ally. This in turn led to a 'Germany-first' strategy in which Germany's destruction took precedence over that of Japan. The United States had the world's largest economy in 1941. It was larger than the combined economies of all Axis powers. The economies of the powers already at war with the Axis in December 1941 were also slightly larger than those of all three major Axis powers (although Russia was not at war with Japan). By involving the United States, Hitler had more than doubled the resources which could be used against Germany.

In the short term, Hitler's decision looked brilliant. It opened vast expanses of the Atlantic to U-boats at a time when US naval and maritime aviation resources were being redeployed to the Pacific. This was critical to German success. Allied air patrols around Britain, Iceland, Gibraltar and West Africa constrained U-boat activity in the second half of 1941.

Lockheed Hudsons on the apron outside Lockheed's Burbank assembly plant in California awaiting delivery to Coastal Command. US aircraft manufacturers supplied a sizeable fraction of Coastal Command's aircraft during the early years of World War II. (AC)

A shipyard worker looks at another shipbuilder through the torpedo-loading hatch of a U-boat under construction. It typically took two years to complete a U-boat after being ordered. Dönitz lacked sufficient U-boats until 1942. (AC)

'The Happy Time' of late 1940 occurred after U-boats' hunting grounds moved out of reach of shore-based Coastal Command aircraft in Britain. As 1941 ended, Dönitz sought similar areas unpatrolled by aircraft.

The Atlantic west of Iceland was a logical location, but prior to 10 December, the German presence there was constrained by the need to avoid confrontations with the United States. That need disappeared with the US becoming a belligerent, changing the whole complexion of the Battle of the Atlantic.

This event – the entry of US forces as active belligerents and the addition of Arctic convoys to Russia – make December a natural stopping point for a book on the Battle of the Atlantic air war. The Battle of the Atlantic, especially the aerial component, was dramatically different from 1942 on. Yet the first 28 months of the Battle of the Atlantic held important lessons, and in many ways presaged the eventual Allied victory.

Its most important lessons were the need to be ready to fight and to be capable of fighting. Both sides started World War II incapable of winning a Battle of the Atlantic – or more precisely an Atlantic trade war.

Germany lacked the U-boats to win a trade war when the conflict began. It had just 57 in commission in 1939. Of these, nearly half were unsuitable for conducting a campaign to sever Britain's supply lines. It had another 57 on order, under construction or fitting out, but Germany's pre-war building plan was inadequate. It ordered 188 U-boats between August 1939 and the end of the year. It also ordered 235 submarines in 1940 and over 300 more in 1941.

The numbers sound impressive. Over the long run, construction did produce enough boats, even with losses, to exceed Dönitz's stated goal of 300 U-boats so that 100 of them could be at sea at any one time. However, for the first two years of the war it averaged nearly a year between the placing of an order and the beginning of construction, and an additional year after starting construction before the boat was commissioned in the *Kriegsmarine.*

The result was that until the spring of 1941, Dönitz typically had a total of only 20–25 U-boats on patrol in Atlantic waters, and in some months was lucky to average 12 boats at sea each day. It was not until June 1941 that the U-boats on patrol in Atlantic waters exceeded the 40 boats patrolling in early September 1939, a total made possible only because Germany had most of its boats at sea before Britain opened hostilities on 3 September. Germany managed to get 53 boats on patrol in the Atlantic in November 1941, but thereafter transfers to the Mediterranean brought those numbers down to the 30s. There were simply too few U-boats to win the tonnage war. It would not be until August 1942 that Dönitz reached 100 U-boats at sea.

Dönitz was further restricted because German leadership failed to realize they were in a total war with Britain until August 1940. Hitler had looked for a negotiated end after the Polish campaign. When that did not happen, Germany invaded France, knocking it out of the war in one month, then sat back to await negotiations with Britain. Hitler even began demobilization. Only after Britain failed to sue for peace did Germany switch to a full wartime economy. Nearly two-thirds of the 1940 U-boat orders were placed from August onwards.

The Saro Lerwick went straight from the drawing board to the production line without prototype testing. Its fatal flaws went unrecognized until it entered service. Yet the alternative was the certainty of keeping obsolescent biplane flying boats in service. (AC)

While Dönitz and the U-boat arm struggled with a lack of resources, Coastal Command combined a lack of resources with bad decisions until 1941. Often bad decisions were imposed on Coastal Command by the Air Ministry, but several were self-imposed.

Some problems were obvious. Coastal Command recognized the inadequacy of the Anson, and began replacing it with the Hudson prior to the war. They were also working to replace the Vildebeest and biplane flying boats. They were successful with the Beaufort and Sunderland, but failed with the Botha and Lerwick.

The Beaufort, Botha and Lerwick, all ordered off the drawing board without a prototype for evaluation, experienced teething problems. This led to a long development time for the Beaufort, and ultimately the cancellation of the Botha and Lerwick. Yet that gamble was worth taking. By the time that funds were allocated for their development, the aircraft they were to replace were obsolete. Skipping the prototype should have saved replacement time.

A grinning Hudson gunner carries two .303 machine guns to his Hudson as a mission starts. While the .303 was light enough to carry, it lacked the penetrating power of the .50 calibre machine gun. (AC)

Coastal Command was willing to fill gaps in its inventory by turning to the United States, most notably with the Hudson and Catalina. The Hudson was a particularly good choice. It filled Coastal Command's expected early-war needs, could be built in large numbers and was unwanted by Bomber Command. It was also not an aircraft used by United States armed forces. Unlike the Catalina, which was desired by the United States Navy, Britain did not compete with the US military for Hudsons.

Coastal Command could also be excused for underestimating the priority that needed to be placed on sinking U-boats prior to and immediately after the war began. Surface raiders, especially auxiliary cruisers disguised to look like merchantmen, were then viewed as a more immediate danger. Once it became apparent the U-boat was a greater threat – U-boats sank ten times the number of merchant ships as did surface warships in 1939 – priorities quickly shifted to the U-boat.

Less excusable was Coastal Command's lack of an effective anti-submarine weapon. Only the Sunderland could carry the available 450lb depth charge in September 1939. The 100lb anti-submarine bomb destroyed more Coastal Command and FAA aircraft (at least four) than U-boats (zero). The 250lb anti-submarine bomb could damage a U-boat enough to keep it from diving, but actually sinking a U-boat with one was unlikely.

Coastal Command and the Royal Navy shared two U-boat kills during 1940. In one case a Sunderland damaged a U-boat with a 250lb bomb, preventing it from submerging and escaping a British destroyer. In the second case a Sunderland's bombs convinced the crew of a U-boat – previously damaged by surface warships and unable to submerge – to scuttle their vessel.

Coastal Command aircraft sighted U-boats 51 times in 1939, leading to 46 attacks, and 107 times in 1940, leading to 77 attacks. Germany lost nine U-boats in 1939 and 24 in 1940 to all causes. If only 10 per cent of attacks had succeeded in sinking a U-boat, their losses would have been 50 per cent higher in 1939 and 33 per cent higher in 1940.

This sounds insignificant, but in January 1940 Germany had only 32 operational U-boats, of which an average of only 14 were on patrol in Atlantic waters daily. In January 1941 there were only 22 operational U-boats, with an average of nine on patrol each day. Starting 1940 with 27 operational U-boats and 1941 with just ten could have preserved 15–25 of the 114 ships sunk by U-boats in 1939, and up to 150 of the 451 sunk by U-boats in 1940.

This failure to sink more U-boats occurred because these bombs were never tested against submarines. They were developed between 1925 and 1927, and only introduced for service in 1931. Introduction was slowed by the Great Depression and the need to economize. It proved a false economy, although not as much as the unwillingness to expend funds and resources to test the bombs against an actual submarine at sea.

While pre-war budgetary cost-cutting explained that failure, there were other issues, revealed by the war, that were less explicable. Coastal Command was famously last in priority of the RAF's combat commands, so much so that it was called the Cinderella Service. This made sense during the war's first year: initially no one realized the threat posed by U-boats. Until the end of the Battle of Britain, Fighter Command had first priority. Even before the fall of France, Britain needed to prepare its home air defences. Afterwards, Britain had to strain every resource to protect itself from invasion.

By September 1940 the threat posed by German naval bases on the French Atlantic coast should have been clear. Britain's U-boat defences had been flanked. Despite this threat, it took until March 1941 before Churchill issued his 'Battle of the Atlantic Directive', prioritizing the fight against the U-boat.

Even then, the resource tap flowed only slowly. The RAF was run by a cadre who believed strategic bombing would win the war unaided. They viewed every aircraft allocated to Coastal Command as one less aircraft available for Bomber Command. The Wellington and Whitley were suited for maritime patrol, yet Bomber Command begrudged every one allocated to

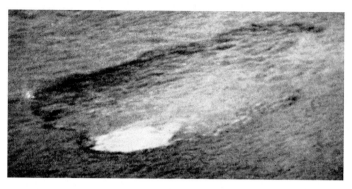

The result of too many Coastal Command attacks between 1939 and 1941 – disturbed water marking a submerging German U-boat successfully evading damage from Coastal Command bombs. (AC)

Coastal Command. Few Wellingtons were allocated to Coastal Command until November 1941, with most converted to detonate magnetic mines (Wellingtons could carry the degaussing loop). Coastal Command then had only one Whitley squadron.

When, in August 1941, Coastal Command requested Wellingtons to equip maritime reconnaissance squadrons, the Air Ministry told it there were no Wellingtons available, even though over 100 were manufactured each month.

Similarly, of the Liberators sent to Britain, Coastal Command received only a handful. The rest were allocated to Bomber Command, which sent most to North Africa where they were used for long-range bombing of African targets. The strategic bombardment of Benghazi and Tripoli may have marginally aided British forces in North Africa, but reallocating two dozen Liberators on those missions to Coastal Command would likely have served them better. They could have slashed losses of cargo ships in the Atlantic. This would have allowed Britain to supply their North African armies with more munitions as fewer cargoes would have been lost. It would also have made more ships available to carry those cargoes, as ships not sunk would have been available for Africa-bound convoys.

Coastal Command also received last call on onboard radars; the Leigh Light, originally developed in September 1940, was not tested until the following spring and did not enter service until January 1942.

The lack of interest in escort carriers was another curiosity. Britain did not attempt to build one until January 1941. HMS *Audacity* proved its worth between September and December 1941, yet it would take until March 1942 for the second one to see action. Except for *Audacity*, all British escort carriers were converted or built in the United States. Britain could have experimented with escort carriers earlier than 1941. HMS *Argus*, built in World War I, was available.

In 1943 Britain added flight decks to nine Royal Dutch Shell oil tankers. Like *Audacity*, they had no hangar decks. Unlike *Audacity*, these nine ships still carried cargoes after conversion, combining the role of tanker and escort carrier. Merchant crews manned the ship: the only naval personnel aboard were the aircrew and maintenance staff. All nine ships were built in the 1930s and were available for conversion in 1940 and 1941.

While Churchill claimed the only thing that ever really frightened him was the U-boat peril, he gave little evidence of that fright in allocation of resources through the first two years of the war.

The years 1939–41 were in effect just a trial run for both sides. The 'real' Battle of the Atlantic would begin in January 1942. Both sides had experienced and battle-hardened people, and effective weapons and tactics. Dönitz eventually was getting the numbers he required, but the Allies finally had the technologies and weapons their aircraft needed to sink U-boats in large numbers. The question was whether the German numbers could overwhelm the Allied convoys before Allied technology contained the U-boats.

## Surviving U-boats and aircraft

No U-boats that saw combat between 1939 and 1941 exist today. The most famous surviving U-boat, U-505, captured by a US Navy hunter-killer group in 1944, was commissioned in August 1941. It went through training until the end of 1941 and departed on its first war patrol on 19 January 1942. It was preserved as a museum ship, and has been on display at the Chicago Museum of Science and Industry in Chicago, Illinois, since March 1954. A Type IXC U-boat, it is the only surviving German U-boat that was in existence between 1939 and 1941.

The only other relevant surviving U-boat is *Vesikko*, a Finnish boat. It was the prototype for the Type IIA U-boat, and served in the Finnish Navy from 1935–45. While all other Finnish submarines were scrapped, *Vesikko* was transferred to Finland's Military Museum. It became open to public display in 1973 and can still be visited at Suomenlinna, Finland.

There are rather more surviving Coastal Command and Fleet Air Arm aircraft of the types used between September 1939 and December 1940. In part this is because many of these aircraft, especially the Avro Anson and Lockheed Hudson, were converted to civilian use after the war. There are nearly two dozen Ansons on static display and three airworthy specimens, including one restored to its Coastal Command appearance. Most are in Canada.

Eleven Hudsons still exist, with three in storage or undergoing restoration, four on static display and one airworthy. Only one is in the UK. The rest are in Commonwealth nations, with six in New Zealand. Nearly a dozen Consolidated B-24 Liberators are preserved in various museums, although none appear to have served in Coastal Command. The Consolidated PBY Catalina has nearly 90 preserved examples, including 24 Canadian-built Cansos, licensed-built copies of the Catalina. The Canso in the Pima Air and Space Museum in Tucson, Arizona, is painted in the colours of RCAF No. 5, formed in 1944 and which participated in the Battle of the Atlantic out of Newfoundland. Similarly, the three Catalinas and Cansos on display in Britain all post-date 1941. No complete Armstrong Whitworth Whitleys survive, and the two surviving Wellingtons were both Bomber Command aircraft

The FAA has fewer surviving examples of aircraft that fought in this period. There are no intact Blackburn Skuas; however, the wrecks of two Skuas that crashed in Norwegian fjords or lakes during the 1940 German invasion were recovered. The wings, fuselage and cockpit of one are on display at the Norwegian aviation museum in Bodø. Twelve Fairey Swordfish currently exist, and three or four are airworthy. Six are on display at various museums: three in Britain, one in Canada, one in Malta and one in Texas. None are known to have operated in the Battle of the Atlantic circa 1939–41.

The best place in Britain to see these aircraft is the Imperial War Museum in Duxford, which has the largest variety of aircraft which fought in the Battle of the Atlantic.

Built in 1943, this Anson was restored to wartime appearance in 2012 and operates out of Wanaka Airport in New Zealand. It is painted in the markings of the RAF's 206 Squadron, which operated Ansons between 1936 and 1940. (Oren Rozen, Wikimedia)

# FURTHER READING

Coastal Command was not only largely forgotten by the Air Ministry and Churchill during World War II, it was generally ignored by historians until the 1990s. It was treated only peripherally in the official histories of the Royal Navy (Roskill) and RAF (Richards). Chris Ashworth's *RAF Coastal Command 1936–1939* (Patrick Stephens Limited, Yeovil, Somerset, 1992) and Andrew Hendrie's *The Cinderella Service: RAF Coastal Command 1939–1945* (Pen & Sword Aviation, Barnsley, South Yorkshire, 2006) then appeared. I relied heavily on both for Coastal Command's story. The Fleet Air Arm's role I pieced together from Roskill and Jones.

The best book I found for the perspective of the U-boats during this period was Clay Blair, Jr's *Hitler's U-boat War: The Hunters, 1939–1942* (Random House, New York, NY, 1992). It is a compendium of facts that does not romanticize the U-boats. I also highly recommend uboat.net (https://www.uboat.net/) as a comprehensive collection on the U-boat war.

For fiction, try Nevil Shute's novel *Landfall: A Channel Story*, published in 1940. Much of it takes place in an Anson squadron stationed on the Channel coast. It was inspired in part by the *Snapper* incident. It has the limitations of a novel written in wartime: the protagonist actually sinks a German U-boat, which was impossible with the bombs carried by Ansons. But it captures the feel of 1939 Coastal Command. Long out of print, it may be found at second-hand bookstores. Readers in Canada (where it is in the public domain) can download an electronic version at https://www.fadedpage.com/.

Other principal sources used for this book were (books marked with an asterisk are available online at https://archive.org/):

Off duty U-boat crew gather in their quarters to listen to a radio broadcast. A U-boat had little spare room. (AC)

Buchanan, A. R., *The Navy's Air War, A Mission Completed*, Harper & Brothers, New York and London (1946)

Jones, Ben (ed), *The Fleet Air Arm in the Second World War, Volume I – 1939–1941, Norway, the Mediterranean and the Bismarck*, Naval Records Society, Farnham, Surrey (2012)

Meier, Friedrich, *Kriegsmarine am Feind*, Verlag Erich Klingmammer, Berlin (1940)*

Moeller, Kevin M., *The Italian Submarine Force in the Battle of the Atlantic: Left in the Dark*, thesis presented to the Faculty of the US Army Command and General Staff College, Fort Leavenworth, Kansas (2014)

Morison, Samuel Eliot, *History of United States Naval Operations in World War II, Volume 1: The Battle of the Atlantic, September 1939–May 1943*, Little, Brown, Boston, Mass (1946)

Richards, Denis, *The Royal Air Force 1939–1945, Vol 1: The Fight at Odds*, Her Majesty's Stationery Office, London (1953)

Roskill, S. W., *History of the Second World War, War at Sea, 1939–45: The Defensive Vol. 1*, Her Majesty's Stationary Office, London (1954)

*War Diary of the German Naval Staff Volumes 1–28 (August, 1939–December 1941)*, Office of Naval Intelligence, Washington, D.C. (1950)*

Wood, Derek (ed.), *Seek and Sink: Bracknell Paper No 2 – A Symposium on the Battle of the Atlantic, 21 October 1991*, The Royal Air Force Historical Society, Bracknell, Berkshire, (1992)

# INDEX